PAINT SHOP PRO 7

in

STEPHEN COPESTAKE

COMPUTER
STEP

In easy steps is an imprint of Computer Step
Southfield Road . Southam
Warwickshire CV47 OFB . England

http://www.ineasysteps.com

Notice of Liability

Every effort has been made to ensure that this book contains accurate and current information. However, Computer Step and the author shall not be liable for any loss or damage suffered by readers as a result of any information contained herein.

Trademarks

Paint Shop Pro™ is a trademark of Jasc Software Incorporated. All other trademarks are acknowledged as belonging to their respective companies.

Printed and bound in the United Kingdom

ISBN 1-84078-130-0

Table Of Contents

Using deformations 127

5

Using effects 139

6

Advanced techniques   165

7

Index   187

First steps

In this chapter, you'll learn how to use the Paint Shop Pro screen (including guides and grids); open existing files; create new ones; save changes to disk; and export images for use on the Web (including rollovers, image slicing and mapping). You'll rescale images, and resize the underlying canvas, then go on to learn about image formats and special screen modes. You'll also zoom in and out on images, and reverse/redo image amendments. Finally, you'll learn how to work with background/foreground colours.

Covers

Chapter One

The Paint Shop Pro screen

The Paint Shop Pro screen is exceptionally easy to use.
When you run the program, this is the result:

Title bar   Menu bar   Toolbar

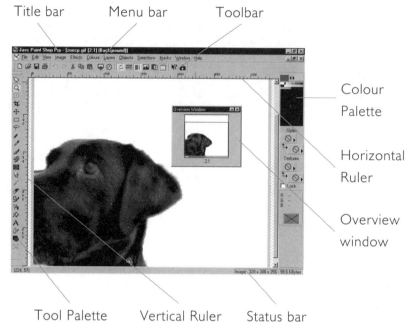

Colour
Palette

Horizontal
Ruler

Overview
window

Tool Palette   Vertical Ruler   Status bar

The other components are common to most or all Windows programs. See your Windows documentation for how to use them.

The Toolbar

This is a collection of icons. By clicking an appropriate icon, you can launch a specific feature.

Many other screen features (e.g. the Status bar, Colour Palette and Overview window) are also classed as toolbars.

For more on the Overview window, see page 28.

The Tool Palette

A specialised toolbar which you use to launch a variety of tools (e.g. the Zoom tool – see page 27).

The Colour Palette

An easy and convenient way to access Paint Shop Pro's colour selection tools (see pages 32-33).

Using guides

You can create guides in Paint Shop Pro pictures. Guides are useful alignment devices because you can ensure that:

- selections

- vector objects

- brush strokes

are automatically aligned with guides when they come within a specific distance.

To specify the distance at which objects snap to guides, double-click a ruler. In the dialog, type in a distance (in pixels) in the Snap influence in pixels field. Click OK.

Creating guides

1 Ensure rulers are currently displayed (see page 11)

2 Ensure guides are currently displayed (see page 11)

3 Click in the vertical or horizontal ruler and drag to produce a guide

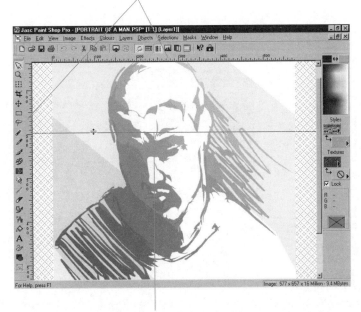

A horizontal guide

You can also have Paint Shop Pro apply a grid to images. Grids are a structure of horizontal/vertical lines which you can use to align objects more accurately:

Part of a grid

To view (or hide) the grid, press Ctrl+Alt+G.

If an image has both guides and a grid active, the grid is ignored.

To delete a guide, drag it off the image window.

To have selections/ vector objects align with guides, the Snap To Guides feature must be turned on. If it isn't, pull down the View menu and click Snap To Guides.

You can perform a variety of editing actions on existing guides.

Moving guides

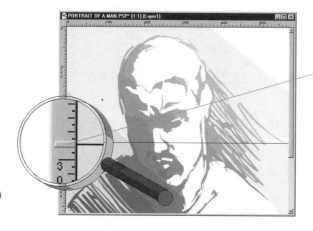

Drag the guide handle to a new location

Recolouring guides

By default, guides are black. To apply a new colour:

1 Double-click a guide's handle

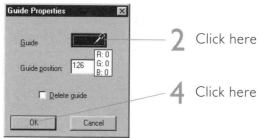

2 Click here

4 Click here

3 Refer to the Colour ring on the top right of the Colour dialog. Drag on the outer ring to select a hue, then drag the selector in the inner square to adjust the saturation. When the New colour box shows the correct colour, click OK

Customising screen components

To view or hide a toolbar, follow step 1 but select Toolbars instead. Do the following:

You can use two techniques to specify which screen components display:

Displaying the grid, guides or rulers

Pull down the View menu and do the following:

B **Click here**

A Select or deselect one or more toolbars

(You can also use this method to hide the Tool and Colour Palettes, or the Overview window.)

Click Grid, Guides or Rulers

Displaying the Tool and Colour palettes

In the on-screen Toolbar, do the following as appropriate:

Step 1 also hides the Grid, Guides or Rulers, as appropriate.

To hide the Status bar, right-click the Tool Palette and select Status Bar.

Click here to show/ hide the Tool palette

Click here to show/ hide the Colour palette

Opening files

If you open a vector format, a second dialog may open after step 2 e.g.:

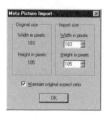

Complete the dialog, then click OK.

Paint Shop Pro will open (i.e. read and display) over 40 separate graphics file formats. These fall into two broad categories: raster and vector – see page 26 for details of some of the principal image formats supported by Paint Shop Pro. When you tell Paint Shop Pro to open an image, it automatically recognises which format it was written to, and acts accordingly. It does this by taking account of the file suffix. For example, for TIFF (Tagged Image File Format) images to be opened in Paint Shop Pro, they must end in:

.TIF

Not all of the supported formats, however, can be written to disk. (See pages 18-24 for how to save/export files.)

You open files via the Open dialog, or via a special Browser.

Opening images – the dialog route

| Pull down the File menu and click Open

Before you carry out step 2, carry out the following procedures:

- *use the Look in: field to locate the drive which hosts the file you want to open, and;*

- *(if necessary) double-click one or more folders until you locate the relevant file*

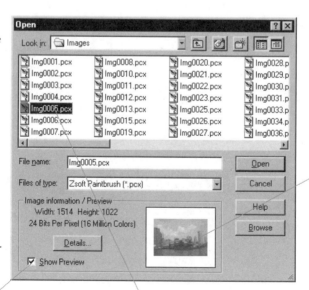

Image Preview

To preview your image before you open it, ensure Show Preview is activated (as here).

2 Double-click a graphics file

Opening images – the Browser route

1 Follow step 1 on the facing page

2 Carry out the procedures in the DON'T FORGET tip on the facing page

3 Click this button: [Browse]

You can also use the Browser for file housekeeping. Do the following:

Press Ctrl+B if the Browser isn't on-screen. Then simply right-click any image thumbnail on the right of the Browser and do any of the following:

- *to rename the image, click Rename. In the Rename File dialog, type in the new name and click OK*

- *to copy the image, click Copy To. In the Browse for Folder dialog, type in the destination folder and click OK, or;*

- *to delete the image, click Delete. In the message which appears, click Yes to confirm the deletion*

- *for brief image details, place the mouse pointer over a thumbnail for a few seconds – an explanatory box launches e.g.:*

```
03.tif
802 x 602 x 16 Million, 65.0 KB
Tagged Image File Format
30/10/2000 16:03:56
```

To close the Browser, press Ctrl+F4.

Image thumbnails

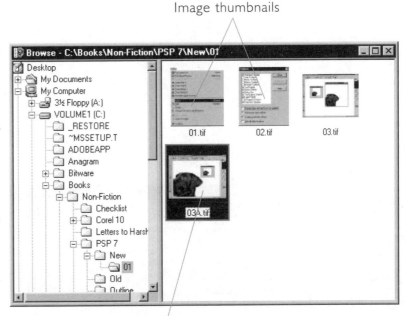

4 Double-click an image

Resizing files

Pixels (a contraction of 'picture element') are dots, the smallest element which can be displayed on screen.
Bitmapped graphics consist of pixels; each is allocated a colour (or greyscale).

Paint Shop Pro lets you resize an image. You can do this in three ways:

- by altering the pixel dimensions

- by restating the dimensions as a percentage of the original

- by changing the image resolution (called 'resampling')

Resizing an image

1. Pull down the Image menu and click Resize

2. Perform step 3, 4 OR 5. Finally, carry out step 6:

3. Click here, then amend the associated Width or Height fields

Re step 5 – increasing the resolution reduces the image size (and vice versa).

To select a new resizing type, click the Resize Type field. In the list, select a type.

Resizing bitmaps produces some level of distortion.
The trick is to minimise this as far as possible.

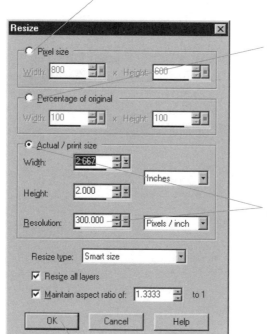

4. Click here, then amend the associated Width or Height fields

5. Click here, then type in a new resolution in the Resolution field

6. Click here

New files

To duplicate the active image, click its Title bar. Press Shift+D; Paint Shop Pro opens the copy in its own (new) window.

Often, images will be 'ready-made' for you, in the sense that you'll:

- open existing images (see pages 12-13)

- create screenshots by carrying out screen captures (see Chapter 7)

- duplicate existing images (see the HOT TIP)

However, there will be times when you'll need to create an image from scratch. There are several stages, but Paint Shop Pro makes this easy:

Resolution is defined as the measurement (usually expressed in linear dpi – dots per inch) of image sharpness.

1. launching the New Image dialog

2. specifying the width and height, in pixels

3. selecting a background colour

4. specifying the resolution

5. selecting an image type (including the number of colours)

Creating a new image

Pull down the File menu and do the following:

This is the version of the File menu which launches if you haven't already opened or created a picture. (If you have, there are more options.)

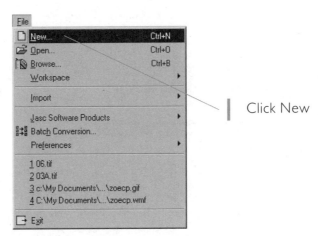

Click New

Now carry out the following steps:

To specify the image resolution, type it in here:

2 Complete the Width and Height fields

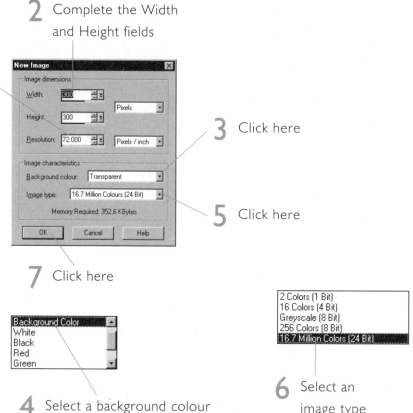

3 Click here

5 Click here

Re the above tip – use the following suggestions as guidelines:

• *Web pictures – use a resolution of 72 pixels per inch, and;*

• *other pictures – use the range 96-150 pixels per inch (this is a useful standard)*

7 Click here

4 Select a background colour

6 Select an image type

The resulting image:

A new, blank image (the background colour is white) in its own window

Enlarging an image's canvas

Note that enlarging an image's canvas (unlike resizing) does not expand the image itself.

As we've seen on pages 15-16, when you create an image from scratch, you specify the width and height in pixels. When you do this, Paint Shop Pro automatically defines a 'canvas' (the area on which the image lies) with the same dimensions. However, you can easily specify increased dimensions for the canvas (e.g. if you resize the image).

Increasing an image's canvas

Before you carry out steps 1-3 here, first follow step 2 under 'Using the Select Colour panel' on page 33 to select a background colour.

1 Pull down the Image menu and click Canvas Size

2 Complete the New Width and/or New Height fields

3 Optional – select either or both of these to centre the image within the new canvas

Re step 3 – if you don't select both centring options, also complete the relevant placement boxes:

Top:	-106
Bottom:	-106
Left:	-146
Right:	-147

Canvas enlargement in action:

Here, the canvas has been enlarged vertically and horizontally

In this instance, the background is white

Saving files

Re step 1 – Paint Shop Pro has its own proprietary format (suffix: .PSP) which retains:

- *layers*
- *vectors*
- *masks*
- *selection data*

Use the PSP format while you're working with an image; when it's complete, save it to the nonproprietary format of your choice.

When you're working on one or more images in Paint Shop Pro, it's important to save your work at frequent intervals, in order to avoid data loss in the event of a hardware fault or power interruption.

Saving a file for the first time

Pull down the File menu and click Save. Now do the following:

2 Click here; in the drop-down list, click a drive

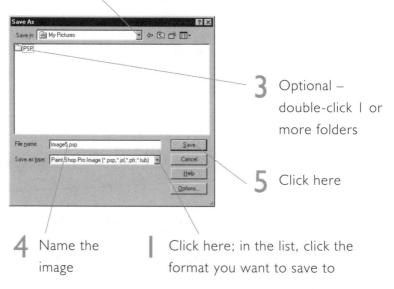

3 Optional – double-click 1 or more folders

5 Click here

4 Name the image

1 Click here; in the list, click the format you want to save to

Re. step 1 – many image formats have sub-formats and/or compression options you can choose from.

If it's available, click this button immediately after step 1:

Options...

In the resulting dialog, select the appropriate option(s). Click OK.

Saving previously saved files

Pull down the File menu and click Save. No dialog launches; instead, Paint Shop Pro saves the latest version of your file to disk, overwriting the previous.

Saving copies of images

You can also save a copy of the active picture (and leave the original intact).

Pull down the File menu and click Save Copy As. Now follow steps 1-5 above.

Exporting files for the Internet

Image formats which are suitable for Web use include:

- *GIF (suitable for line art and images of 256 colours or fewer)*
- *JPEG (especially effective for photographs)*
- *PNG (suitable for most images, but not supported by all browsers)*

See page 26 for more information.

You can use steps 1-5 on the facing page to produce files suitable for Internet use. However, Paint Shop Pro makes it even easier to produce transparent GIF, JPEG and PNG files by providing specialised export dialogs.

Exporting GIF/JPEG/PNG files

1 Pull down the File menu and click Export

2 In the sub-menu, click JPEG Optimizer, GIF Optimizer or PNG Optimizer

3 Complete the dialog which launches (the dialog varies according to which option is chosen in step 2):

No browsers currently support layers. Therefore, before you export a layered picture for Web use, flatten it by pulling down the Layers menu and selecting Merge, Merge All (Flatten).

4 Activate each tab in turn, then complete the relevant options

Consider limiting Web images to a maximum of 256 colours to avoid distortion ("dithering") in browsers on PCs which do not support more.

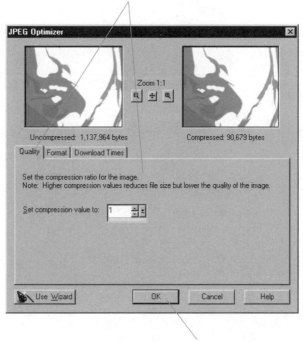

5 Click here

Exporting GIF/JPEG/PNG files – a simpler route

If you're unsure about completing all of the options when you export files for Internet use (and some of the options – particularly PNG – can be complex), you can use a shortcut:

Smaller file sizes work better on the Web (many users won't wait while large files download). So effective publishing on the Web involves getting the maximum compression while keeping image quality adequately high.

1 Follow steps 1-2 on the previous page

2 Click this button in the dialog: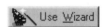

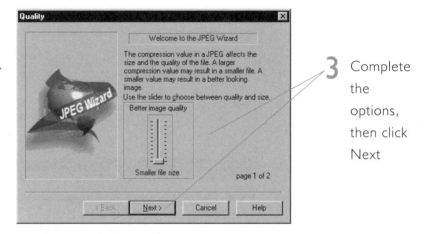

3 Complete the options, then click Next

4 Complete any further dialogs which launch (clicking Next where applicable to move on to the next dialog)

5 In the Final dialog, click Finish to complete the export process

Image slicing

You can use a technique known as image slicing to:

- save an image into smaller parts (in various formats/ specifications)

- reduce downloading time (by saving fewer image parts – those used repeatedly are only saved the once)

1 Select the image you want to split

2 Pull down the File menu and click Export, Image Slicer

3 Click one of these, then click in the image preview

To delete a cell, do the following. Click this button in the dialog:

Now click the cell.

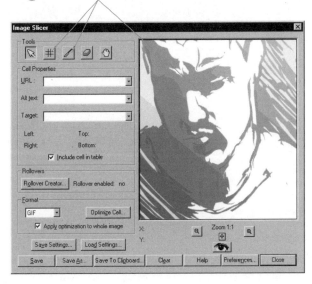

The Image Slicer works by dividing images into rectangles. You do this by applying grids (step 4) or lines (step 5).

When you've done this, you apply specific properties to the rectangles (cells) – see page 22.

4 If you selected ▦ in step 3, complete the Grid Size dialog, then click OK

5 If you selected ✎ in step 3, click and drag vertically over the image preview to create a vertical line, or horizontally to create a horizontal line

6 Click here, then select a cell (it's outlined in green)

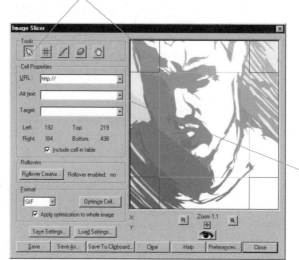

To preview your image in your Internet browser, click this button:

7 Complete the Properties section

8 Click in the Format box and select a format (e.g. GIF)

9 Click **Optimize Cell...** and complete the dialog which launches by activating each tab and selecting the relevant options in each

10 Click Close and complete any further dialogs

The image previewed in Internet Explorer 5.5 (here, for illustration purposes, the quality isn't quite right)

Using rollovers

You can also use Paint Shop Pro 7 to export "rollovers". Rollovers are image sections which change into something else when activated and are often used on the Internet, particularly in Web site navigation bars.

The use of rollovers can make Web sites look much more graphically effective, and more professional.

Exporting rollovers

1 Follow steps 1-6 on pages 21-22

2 Click this button: Rollover Creator...

3 Select the appropriate initiating mouse action

Repeat steps 3-5 as often as required.

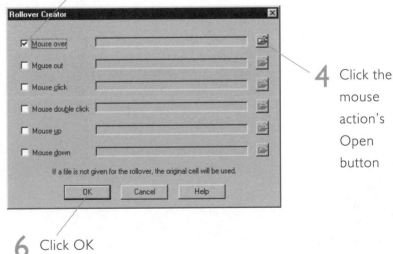

4 Click the mouse action's Open button

6 Click OK

5 Use the Open dialog to locate the graphics file you want to associate with the rollover

Image mapping

You can use a technique known as image mapping to create image areas (hot spots) which are linked to Internet addresses (URLs):

1 Select the image you want to map

To delete a shape you've defined in step 4, do the following.

Click this button:

Now click the shape.

2 Pull down the File menu and click Export, Image Mapper

3 Click the Polygon, Rectangle or Circle tool, then click in the image preview

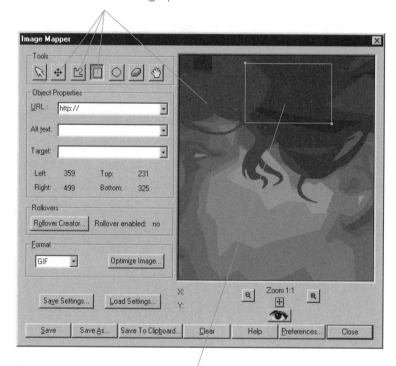

The Image Mapper works by dividing images into polygons, rectangles or circles.

When you've done this, you apply specific properties to the shapes – see page 25.

4 Drag out a map shape

...cont'd

5 Click here, then select a shape (it's outlined in green)

To apply a rollover to the mapped area, click the Rollover Creator button. (For how to proceed now, see page 23.)

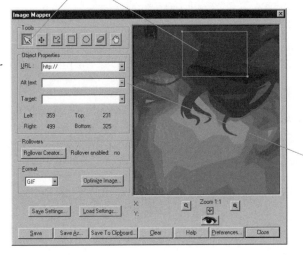

6 Complete the Properties section

To preview your image in your Internet browser, click this button:

7 Click in the Format box and select a format (e.g. GIF)

8 Click  and complete the dialog which launches by activating each tab and selecting the relevant options in each

9 Click Close and complete any further dialogs

The image previewed in Internet Explorer 5.5 (here, for illustration purposes, the quality isn't quite right)

Brief notes on image formats

Image formats supported by Paint Shop Pro are bitmaps (rasters), vectors and metas.

Bitmaps consist of coloured dots, while vectors are defined by equations (thus often giving better results with rescaled images). Metas are blanket formats which explicitly allow the inclusion of raster and vector data, as well as text annotations.

Another bitmap format – JPEG (Joint Photographic Experts Group) – is used for photograph storage, especially on the Internet. It supports a very high-level of compression, usually without appreciable distortion.

Another bitmap format used occasionally on the Web is Interlaced Portable Network Graphics (suffix: .PNG).

An example of a meta format is Windows Metafile (suffix: .WMF). This can be used for data exchange between just about all Windows programs.

Paint Shop Pro will import a wide selection of bitmap, vector and meta graphic formats. These are some of the main ones:

Bitmap formats

PCX — Originated with PC Paintbrush. Used for years to transfer graphics data between Windows application. Supports compression

TIFF — Tagged Image File Format. Suffix: .TIF. If anything, even more widely used than PCX, across a whole range of platforms and applications

BMP — Not as common as PCX and TIFF, but still popular. Tends to produce large files

TGA — Targa. A high-end format, and also a bridge with so-called low-end computers (e.g. Amiga and Atari). Often used in PC and Mac paint and ray-tracing programs because of its high-resolution colour fidelity. Supports compression

GIF — Graphics Interchange Format. Just about any Windows program – and a lot more besides – will read GIF. Frequently used on the Internet. Disadvantage: it can't handle more than 256 colours. Compression is supported

PCD — (Kodak) PhotoCD. Used primarily to store photographs on CD. Paint Shop Pro will not export to PCD

Vector formats

CGM — Computer Graphics Metafile. Frequently used in the past, especially as a medium for clip-art transmission. Less frequently used nowadays

EPS — The most widely used PostScript format. Combines vector and raster data with a low-resolution informational bitmap header. The preferred vector format

Zoom

Paint Shop Pro uses a simple nomenclature to denote what happens when you zoom in or out.

For example, an image at its normal view level is described as:

1:1

If you zoom in three times, this is shown as:

3:1

Alternatively, if you zoom out six times, this is shown as:

1:6

(You can zoom in to 32:1, and out to 1:24.)

The ability to 'zoom in' (magnify) or 'zoom out' (reduce magnification) is very important when you're working with images in Paint Shop Pro. When you zoom in or out, Paint Shop Pro increases or reduces the magnification by single increments.

1 Click this button in the Tool Palette:

2 Place the mouse pointer where you want to zoom in or out

You can also use another technique to zoom in. Follow steps 1-2. Now hold down the left mouse button and drag to define the area you want to enlarge. Finally, release the mouse button.

3 Left-click to zoom in, OR right-click to zoom out

Re step 3 – you should repeat this as often as necessary.

The result of zooming in

The Overview window

When you've zoomed in on part of an image, Paint Shop Pro lets you view the entire image at the same time. You do this by launching the Overview window. This is a very useful feature, though it does have one disadvantage: it may result in Paint Shop Pro operating more slowly.

Launching the Overview window

To launch the Overview window, pull down the View menu and click Toolbars. In the dialog, click Overview Window, Close.

Using the Overview window

Do the following:

To hide the Overview window, repeat this procedure.

JASC, the manufacturers of Paint Shop Pro, have their own Web site. You can use this to:

- *download a free, 30-day trial version of Paint Shop Pro 7*

- *upgrade existing installations of Paint Shop Pro*

- *download other JASC software – including WebDraw, the SVG (Scalable Vector Graphics) editor. (SVG, a new Web graphics format) looks set to be very popular in the near future.*

JASC's Web address is:

http://www.jasc.com

If an image is being viewed at a high magnification and not all of it displays in its window, the Overview window shows a rectangle representing the visible area. Drag this to view a new area

Full Screen Preview mode

Paint Shop Pro also has another view mode: Full Screen Edit.

This hides:

- *the Title bar*
- *the Menu bar, and;*
- *the Status bar*

To launch (or leave) Full Screen Edit mode, press Shift+A.

Paint Shop Pro has a special screen mode which shows the current image (minus other screen components) set against a black background.

Use Full Screen Preview mode to preview changes you've made (and as a preliminary to running the more detailed Print Preview mode – see chapter 7).

Entering Full Screen Preview mode

Pull down the View menu and click Full Screen Preview.

An image in
Full Edit mode

An image
viewed
normally

To leave Full Screen Preview, press Esc.

The same
image in Full
Screen
Preview
mode

Undo and Revert

You can undo more than one action at a time.

Ignore step 1 on the right. Instead, pull down the Edit menu and click Command History. Do the following:

Paint Shop Pro has two features which, effectively, allow you to revert to the way things were *before* you carried out one or more amendments to the active image.

The Undo command

You can 'undo' (i.e. reverse) the last editing action by issuing a menu command.

Pull down the Edit menu and do the following:

A Click an undo level

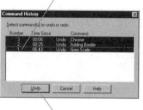

B Click here

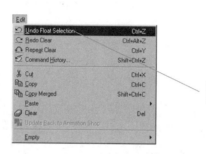

I Click Undo ... (the ellipses denote the action being undone)

Repeat step 1 to undo subsequent actions.

(Note that selecting a lower undo level automatically selects levels above it).

The Revert command

You can – in a single command – undo all the editing changes made to an image since it was last saved. You do this by having Paint Shop Pro abandon the changes and reopen the last-saved version of the file.

Pull down the File menu and do the following:

You can turn off undos if you want. Pull down the File menu and click Preferences, General Program Preferences. Activate the Undo/Redo tab and click Enable the undo system. Click OK.

(Repeat this to reactivate undos.)

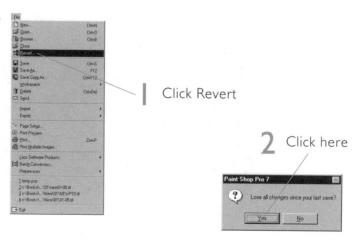

I Click Revert

2 Click here

Redo

You can redo more than one action at a time.
Ignore step 1 on the right. Instead, pull down the Edit menu and click Command History. Do the following:

Paint Shop Pro also lets you undo undoes. This is called 'redoing' an action

The Redo command

You can 'undo' (i.e. reverse) the last editing action by issuing a menu command.

Pull down the Edit menu and do the following:

A Click a redo level

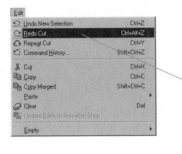

Click Redo ... (the ellipses denote the action being redone)

B Click here

(Clicking a higher redo level automatically selects levels below it).

Redoing in action:

Repeat step 1 to redo subsequent actions.

The Kaleidoscope effect has been applied and then 'undone'...

See chapter 6 for how to apply effects

The result of 'redoing' it

Background/foreground colours

The Colour Palette is normally fixed on the right of the screen. However, it can have an independent existence. To achieve this, double-click anywhere in the Select Colour panel (outside the colours). Now drag the Palette to a new location.

(To reverse this, double-click the Title bar.)

Paint Shop Pro uses two broad colour definitions (called 'active' colours):

Foreground colours — these occupy image foregrounds and are invoked with the left mouse button

Background colours — these occupy image backgrounds and are invoked with the right mouse button

The way you work with foreground and background colours is crucial to your use of Paint Shop Pro. Fortunately, selecting the appropriate colours – via the on-screen Colour Palette – is very easy and straightforward.

The Colour Palette defined

The Colour Palette has the following sections:

If you're working with images with fewer than 16 million colours, Paint Shop Pro 7 only displays 256 colours in the Select Colour panel. This means that when you select a colour, Paint Shop Pro uses that colour which is nearest to the one selected.

(You may find it useful to have the Select Colour panel only display the available 256 colours. To do this, pull down the File menu and click Preferences, General Program Preferences. In the dialog, select the Dialogs and Palettes tab. Activate Show document palette. Click OK.)

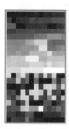

Document palette display

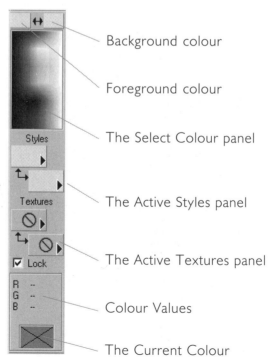

Background colour

Foreground colour

The Select Colour panel

The Active Styles panel

The Active Textures panel

Colour Values

The Current Colour

Using the Select Colour panel

Move the mouse pointer over any active area in the Select Colour Panel. The pointer changes to:

Move the pointer over the colours in the Select Colour Panel; as you do so, the details in the Current Colour box update automatically. When you find the colour you want to use, do ONE of the following:

1 Left-click once to select it as a foreground colour

2 Right-click once to select it as a background colour

You can now go on to combine the selected foreground or background colours with:

*   patterns (called styles)

*   gradients (called styles)

*   textures

Selecting styles

To select and apply a pattern, follow the relevant procedures on pages 80-81.

To select and apply a gradient, follow steps 1-7 on pages 82-83.

Selecting textures

To select and apply a texture, follow steps 1-7 on pages 84-85.

If you don't want to apply a gradient, texture or pattern in addition to foreground/ background colours, carry out step 1 OR 2. Now click the arrow in the relevant Style or Textures box and click the following icons (respectively) in the fly-out:

Solid colour

Null texture

The upper Styles and Textures boxes display the foreground stroke/texture, the lower boxes the background fill/ texture.

Use the left mouse button to apply foreground effects, and the right to apply background effects. (This does not apply to the Shape, Text and Line tools.)

The Clear command

You can have Paint Shop Pro automatically replace an image (or a selection within an image) with the current background colour.

Using Clear

1 Set the relevant background colour via the Colour Palette (see pages 32-33)

2 Optional – define the appropriate selection area (see chapter 2 for how to do this)

3 Pull down the Edit menu and click Clear

Clearing in action:

A selection area has been defined

The selection area after a Clear operation

Making selections

Here, you'll learn about selection types. You'll define rectangular, square, elliptical and circular bitmap selections, then select/group previously created vector objects. You'll also deselect, invert and move selections, then amend feathering. Finally, you'll save selections for reuse later and create multiple/subtractive selections.

Covers

Chapter Two

Selections – an overview

The types on the right are bitmap (raster) selections. However, you can also select vector objects you've created earlier – see page 46.

Selecting all or part of a Paint Shop Pro image is the essential preliminary for performing any of the many supported editing operations.

You can make the following kinds of selections:

- rectangular

- square

- elliptical

- circular

- freehand

To select the whole of the active image in one go, simply press Ctrl+A. (This also selects vector objects.)

- colour-based

- additive and subtractive

Additionally, you can select an entire image in one operation.

Once part of an image has been selected, you can perform the following, selection-specific operations:

You can convert ('promote') raster and vector selections into raster layers (but note that the part of the new layer not containing the selection is transparent). Simply pull down the Selections menu and click Promote to Layer.
For more information on layers, see chapter 7.

— changing selection modes

— removing (deselecting) selections

— inverting bitmap selections

— moving parts of an image

— amending bitmap feathering (the degree of hardness with which the selection is drawn)

— specifying a transparent colour (as a means of limiting selections)

You can also save image selections to disk as special files (and then reopen them at will within other images) and group/ungroup vector selections.

Selection borders

Selected vector objects (see chapter 3 for how to create them) have unbroken borders interspersed with nodes e.g.:

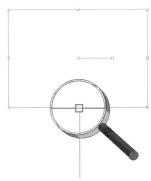

An Edit node – see chapter 3

There are occasions when it's useful to hide selection marquees – for instance, when you've applied feathering and want to see the result more clearly. Note that hiding marquees does not cancel the selection; it's still there.
To hide the active selection's marquee, pull down the Selections menu and click Hide Marquee.
(Repeat to reverse this.)

Generally, whenever you make a bitmap selection in Paint Shop Pro, you'll select *part* of an image. Whether you do this or select an image in its entirety, the portion you've selected is surrounded with a dotted line:

A magnified view of
the selection border

A rectangular
selection

The selection border (sometimes called a 'marquee') moves, which makes it very easy to locate.

Selection modes

To float a selection, press Ctrl+F. To defloat a selection (return it to Standard), press Ctrl+Shift+F.

You can use two kinds of bitmap selection:

Standard   These form part of the original image. In other words, if you move a selection area (see pages 49-50), Paint Shop Pro fills the resultant gap with the background colour

Floating   When a selection area is 'floating', the contents are deemed to be on top of (and distinct from) the original

Floating/ defloating does not apply to vector objects.

Floating v. Standard selections:

If you float a selection on a vector layer (see chapter 7 for more information on layers), it is rasterised.

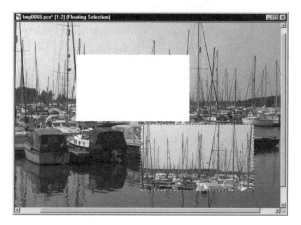

A Standard selection. The selection has been moved, filling the gap with the active background

If you hold down Alt as you drag a Standard selection, it is automatically floated.

A Floating selection. As above, but the underlying image is unaffected

Creating rectangular selections

You can create rectangular bitmap selections in two ways:

If the Tool Options toolbar isn't on-screen, right-click the Tool Palette and select Tool Options in the menu.

- with the use of the mouse

- with the use of a special dialog

The mouse route

Ensure the Tool Palette is on-screen (if it isn't, right-click any toolbar – in the menu, select Tool Palette). Then carry out the following steps:

Re step 2 – if the Tool Options toolbar is on-screen but only its Title bar displays:

Tool Options - Selection ☑ ☒

move the mouse pointer over the Title bar to make the rest of the window appear.

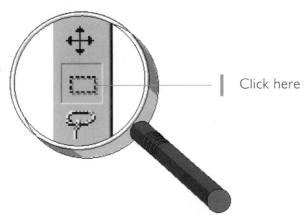

Click here

2 Refer to the Tool Options toolbar and do the following:

To specify the amount of feathering (the sharpness of the selection), type in a value in the Feather: field. Note the following range:

- *0 – maximum sharpness*

- *200 – maximum softness*

3 Ensure this tab is active

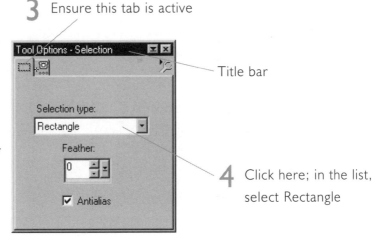

Title bar

4 Click here; in the list, select Rectangle

Note that the Rectangle and Square selection cursor looks like this:

To create a square selection with the mouse, follow steps 1-3 on page 39. In step 4, select Square instead. Now carry out steps 5-6 on the right.

5 Place the mouse pointer at the corner of the area you want to select

6 Drag to define the selection, then release the mouse button

The dialog route

Refer to the Tool Palette and do the following:

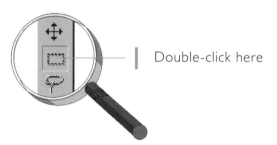

Double-click here

To create a square selection via a dialog, follow the steps on the right (in step 2, type in the appropriate pixel positions).

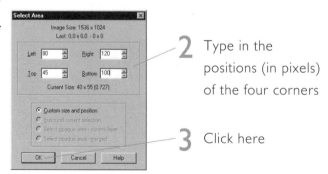

2 Type in the positions (in pixels) of the four corners

3 Click here

Creating elliptical selections

Re step 1 – if the Tool Options toolbar is on-screen but only its Title bar displays:

Tool Options - Selection

move the mouse pointer over the Title bar to make the rest of the window appear.

To create a circular selection, follow step 1 on the right. In step 2, however, select Circle. Now carry out steps 3-5.

1 Perform steps 1-3 on page 39

2 In step 4 on page 39, select Ellipse

3 Place the mouse pointer at the corner of the area you want to select

4 Drag to define the selection

5 Release the mouse button when you've finished

Irregular selections

You can use a special Paint Shop Pro tool – the Freehand tool – to create selections by hand.

Creating freehand selections

Ensure the Tool Palette is on-screen (if it isn't, right-click any toolbar – in the menu, select Tool Palette). Then do the following:

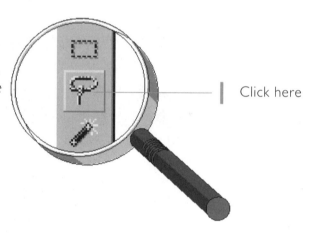

Click here

2 Refer to the Tool Options toolbar and do the following:

3 Ensure this tab is active

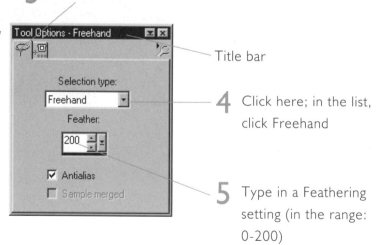

Title bar

4 Click here; in the list, click Freehand

5 Type in a Feathering setting (in the range: 0-200)

The Freehand cursor looks like this:

You can contract or expand bitmap selections uniformly (the shape is retained) via a dialog.

Pull down the Selections menu and click Modify, Contract or Modify, Expand. In the Number of pixels: field in the dialog which launches, type in the extent of the contraction or expansion (in pixels). Click OK.

You can also expand a selection (but only in images with 16 million colours or more) to include contiguous and similar colours.

Pull down the Selections menu and click Modify, Grow Selection.

(Note that this feature uses the Magic Wand tool settings – see steps 3-4 on page 44.)

6 Place the mouse pointer at the location where you want the selection to begin

Skyrides.jpg [1:1] (Background)

7 Drag to define the selection

8 Release the mouse button when you've finished

Selections based on colour

If the Tool Options toolbar isn't on-screen, right-click the Tool Palette and select Tool Options in the menu.

You can use another Paint Shop Pro tool – the Magic Wand – to select portions of the active image which share a specific colour.

Creating colour-based selections

Ensure the Tool Palette is on-screen (if it isn't, right-click any toolbar – in the menu, select Tool Palette). Then do the following:

Re step 2 – if the Tool Options toolbar is on-screen but only its Title bar displays:

`Tool Options - Selection`

move the mouse pointer over the Title bar to make the rest of the window appear.

Click here

2 Refer to the Tool Options toolbar and do the following:

3 Ensure this tab is active

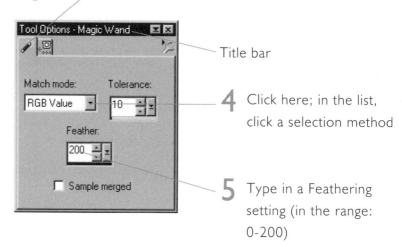

Type in a value in the Tolerance field. (Tolerance is the degree to which image pixels must approach the chosen one to activate selection.) Use this range:

- *0 – only exact matches result in selection*

- *200 – all pixels are selected*

Title bar

4 Click here; in the list, click a selection method

5 Type in a Feathering setting (in the range: 0-200)

The Magic Wand cursor looks like this:

You can also expand a selection (but only in images with 16 million colours or more) to include non-contiguous and similar colours.

Pull down the Selections menu and click Modify, Select Similar.

(Note that this feature uses the Magic Wand tool settings – see steps 3-4 on the facing page.)

To remove a specific colour from an existing selection, follow steps 1-5 on the facing page. Now hold down Ctrl as you click the colour.

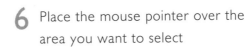

6 Place the mouse pointer over the area you want to select

7 Left-click once

The end result:

The new selection area

Vector selections

To select vector objects you've already created, carry out the following procedure.

Selecting one or more vector objects

See chapter 3 for how to create vector objects.

| Refer to the Tool Palette and do the following:

2 Click here

Re step 3 – to select more than one vector object, hold down Shift as you click them.

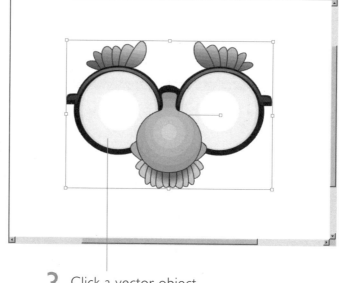

3 Click a vector object (or its outline)

Deselecting selections

You can disable all selections you've already made in two ways:

However, to deselect all vector selections, press Ctrl+D instead. Or, if this tool is active in the Tool Palette:

simply left-click outside a selection.

The menu route

Pull down the Selections menu and do the following:

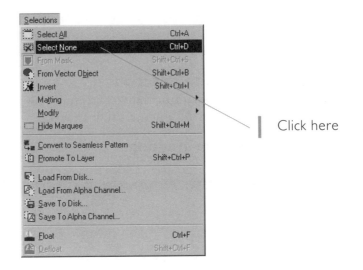

Click here

The mouse route

Provided one of these Tool Palette tools is active:

you can do the following:

Within the active image, right-click once

Inverting selections

When you've selected a portion of an image, you can have Paint Shop Pro do BOTH of the following:

When you invert freehand selections, Paint Shop Pro may not display the inversion accurately. However, any editing changes you make to the selected area will display correctly.

- deselect the selected area

- select the external area which was previously unselected

Paint Shop Pro calls this 'inverting a selection'. Use inversion as a means of creating selections which would otherwise be difficult – or impossible – to achieve.

Inverting a selection

First make a normal selection. Then pull down the Selections menu and click Invert.

Inversion in action:

In the lower figure, Paint Shop Pro has also surrounded the selected area (here, the image minus the additive selection) with a dotted border:

An additive selection (see page 55)

After inversion – the marquee now encloses the *unselected* area

Moving selections

To move a vector object, ensure this Tool Palette tool is active:

Now click the object's outline. Keep the pointer on the outline until it looks like this:

Hold down the left mouse button and drag the object to a new location. Release the mouse button.

Paint Shop Pro lets you move bitmap selections (by detaching them from the host layer). You can:

- move just the frame which defines the selection area

OR

- move the frame AND the contents

Moving selection frames only

Refer to the Tool Palette and do the following:

Click here

Ensure the selection frame has not been made floating (see page 38) before carrying out the procedures here.

2 Right-click inside the existing selection area, then drag it to a new location

Moving selection frames in action:

The irregular selection area from the facing page has been moved

You can also move selections and their contents with the keyboard.

Hold down Shift. Now press and hold down any of the cursor keys.

(Hold down Ctrl as well as Shift to increase the move speed.)

The procedures in the above tip also apply to selected vector objects (except that the underlying image is unaffected).

An advanced user's tip – hold down Ctrl and Alt while pressing any of the arrow keys to:

• *copy the selection (leaving the original unaffected)*

• *move it one pixel at a time*

simultaneously.

When you move a Standard selection, the original area is filled with the active background colour.

Moving bitmap selection frames and contents

First, ensure that the selection area is Standard or Floating, according to the effect you want to achieve. (See page 38 for a description of the two possible effects). Then:

1 In the Tool Palette, activate the tool which was used to create the selection

2 Drag the selection to a new location

Moving selection contents in action:

Moving the contents of a Standard selection

Moving the contents of a Floating selection

Amending selection feathering

Re step 1 – feathering is the sharpness of the selection. Note the range:

- *0 – maximum sharpness*
- *200 – maximum softness*

Moving selections (see pages 49-50) leaves some of the surrounding pixels attached to the selection border:

As we've seen, when you define a selection within an image, you have the opportunity to customise the feathering. However, you can also do this (and to a greater extent) *after* the selection area has been created.

Imposing a new feathering

Define a selection. Pull down the Selections menu and click Modify, Feather. Now do the following:

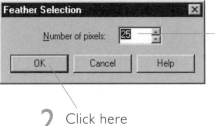

Feather Selection

Number of pixels: 25

OK   Cancel   Help

Type in a new feathering

2 Click here

Re-feathering in action:

A magnified view of the feathered selection edge

Unwanted pixels

Img0023.pcx* [1:1]

The pixels have been removed

To achieve this, ensure the selection is floating. Click Selections, Matting. Then click Defringe, Remove White Matte or Remove Black Matte, as appropriate.

This square selection has been dragged to the right

Selecting a transparent colour

The Remove Selected Colour dialog only lets you select a few basic colours.

For more precision, though, follow the procedures on page 33 to select a specific background or foreground colour, then select Foreground Colour or Background Colour in step 1. Finally, follow step 2.

You can specify a transparent colour; this tells Paint Shop Pro to deselect it within a selection.

Selecting a colour

Define a selection. Pull down the Selections menu and click Modify, Transparent Colour. Now do the following:

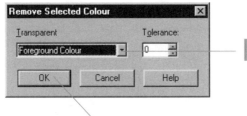

Click here; in the list, select a colour

2 Click here

Also type in a value in the Tolerance field. (Tolerance is the degree to which image pixels must approach the chosen one to activate selection.) Use this range:

- *0 – only exact matches result in selection*

- *200 – all pixels are selected*

Transparent colour selection in action:

In this example, a rectangular selection was made around the turret, then one of the turret colours was selected as the Foreground colour (with a fairly low tolerance) using the technique discussed in the HOT TIP at the top of the page. In step 1, Foreground Colour was selected. Then, when the frame was moved to the left, all colours apart from the foreground were moved.

Moving this selection area illustrates transparent colour selection – see the DON'T FORGET tip

Reusing selections

Paint Shop Pro lets you save a selection area (the frame, NOT the contents) to disk, as a special file. You can then load it into a new image. This is a convenient way to reuse complex selections.

An unusual selection, saved to disk...

See pages 55-56 for how to create selections like this.

... and then loaded into another image

Selection files have the suffix: .SEL

Saving a selection

Define a selection. Pull down the Selections menu and click Save To Disk. Now do the following:

| Click here; in the drop-down list, select a drive

Re step 1 – you may also have to double-click one or more folders first, to locate the folder you want to save the selection to.

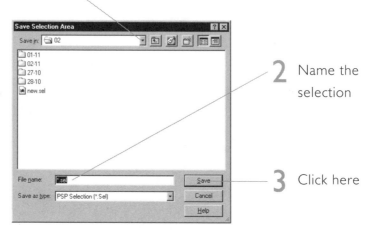

2 Name the selection

3 Click here

Loading a selection

Pull down the Selections menu and click Load From Disk. Now do the following:

Re step 1 – you may also have to double-click one or more folders first, to locate the folder which hosts the relevant selection file.

| Click here; in the drop-down list, select a drive

2 Double-click a selection

Selection additions/subtractions

When you create multiple selections, a plus sign is added to the cursor for the relevant tool. For example, the Rectangle selector looks like this:

You can define multiple (additive) selections. This is a very useful technique which enables you to create spectacular effects. You can also create selections subtractively, where Paint Shop Pro decreases the size of a selection in line with further contiguous selections you define.

Creating multiple (additive) selections

| Define the first selection, using any of the techniques previously discussed:

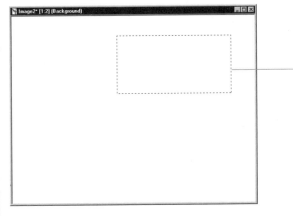

Here, a rectangular selection has been created

Re step 2 – if (as here) you define a further selection which encroaches onto the first, the two are joined. If, on the other hand, you define the second selection so that it does not touch the first, this creates two separate selections:

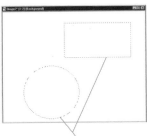

Two independent selections

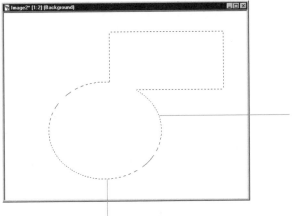

A further elliptical selection has been defined (forming one unusual selection)

Re step 2 – if you're using the Magic Wand to create multiple selections, simply hold down Shift as you click the area you want to add.

2 Hold down Shift, then define another selection

Creating subtractive selections

When you perform selection subtractions, Paint Shop Pro adds a minus sign to the cursor for the relevant selection tool. For example, the Rectangle selector looks like this:

| Define the first selection, using any of the techniques previously discussed:

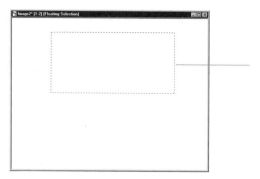

Here, a rectangular selection has been created

Re step 2 – if you're using the Magic Wand tool, simply hold down Ctrl as you click within the first selection area – Paint Shop Pro subtracts the second selection from the first.

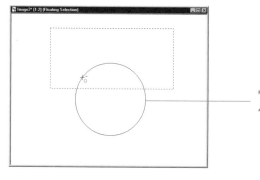

2 Hold down Ctrl as you define another contiguous selection

3 Release the mouse button

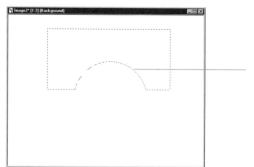

Paint Shop Pro has 'subtracted' the second selection from the first

Grouping/ungrouping

Paint Shop Pro lets you organise vector objects into 'groups'. When grouped, objects can be manipulated jointly in the normal way (for instance, you can save/load them.)

Grouping vector objects

Grouping vectors automatically moves them to the same layer.

1 First select all the relevant vector objects (see page 46 for how to do this)

You can have groups within groups (up to 100 levels). This is called 'nesting'.

2 Pull down the Objects menu and click Group

To ungroup a group, select it. Then pull down the Objects menu and select UnGroup.

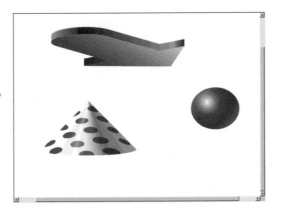

Ungrouped vector objects

Here, all three objects were selected by clicking just one with the Object Selector tool – 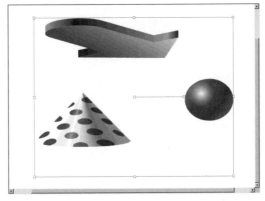 *– active.*

Grouped vector objects

...cont'd

Removing grouped vector objects

You can remove single objects from groups.

1 If the Layer palette isn't on screen, right click any toolbar. In the menu, click Layer palette.

4 Drag the vector to a new layer (as here) or group

If necessary, first click here to display all layers.

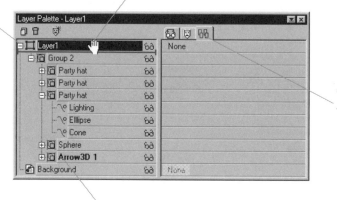

2 Click here

3 Click a group member

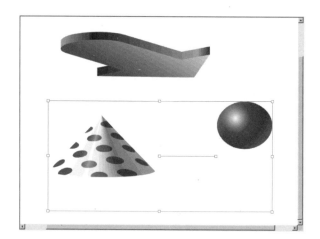

Now, the arrow is no longer part of the group

Painting and drawing

In this chapter, you'll learn how to create a variety of painting/drawing effects. You'll perform freehand painting; copy colours; carry out colour substitutions; select specific colours for foreground/background use; retouch images; carry out spray painting; fill images with colours, patterns, other images, gradients and textures; and paint with object collections (picture tubes). Finally, you'll format and insert text; create lines and preset shapes (including saving them to a library for future use); then reshape them by moving their nodes.

Covers

Chapter Three

Painting and drawing – an overview

Paint Shop Pro lets you paint and draw on-screen, using a variety of specialised but easy to use tools located within the Tools Palette.

With many of the operations in this chapter, you can restrict the effect to specific image parts by using selection areas or masks.

You can:

- create freehand paintings/drawings

- copy colours within images

- carry out colour substitutions (globally and manually)

- carry out image retouching (the manual application of special effects to images or image selections)

- carry out spray painting/drawing

For information on how to include patterns, textures or gradients in operations you perform with the Paintbrush tool, see page 33.

- fill images with colours

- fill images with patterns (or other images)

- fill images with textures

- fill images with gradients

- insert raster or vector text into images

- edit/format existing vector text

- apply vector text onto vector object outlines

- create single, freehand and Bezier lines/curves

- create preset shapes (circles, ellipses, squares, rectangles, triangles or more complex shapes)

- save vectors you create to a 'library', for future use

- paint with object collections (called 'picture tubes')

- reshape vector objects by manipulating their nodes (you can also create your own), handles and contours

Painting with the Paintbrush tool

To launch the Tool Options toolbar, right-click the Tool palette; in the menu, click Tool Options.

Re step 4 – you should make use of the following guidelines:

- *Shape – select a shape (e.g. Square or Horizontal)*

- *Size – select a brush size in pixels (in the range 1-255)*

- *Hardness – select a % in the range 0-100*

- *Opacity – select a % in the range 1-100 (100 is maximum opacity)*

- *Step (mimics brush contact) – select a % in the range 1-100*

- *Density – select a % in the range 1-100*

Re step 6 – you should carry out one of the following operations:

- *drag with the left mouse button to paint with the active foreground colour/ style/texture (see page 33), or;*

- *drag with the right mouse button to paint with the active background colour/ style/texture*

Creating a painting

Refer to the Tool palette and do the following:

| Click here

2 Refer to the Tool Options toolbar and do the following:

3 Ensure this tab is active

4 Complete these fields

5 Place the mouse pointer where you want to start painting

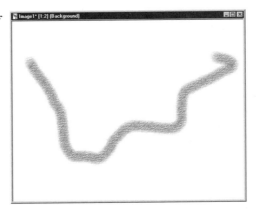

6 Define the painting, then release the mouse button

Drawing with the Paintbrush tool

Drawing lines

Refer to the Tool palette and do the following:

| Click here

You can also use the Draw tool to draw lines – see pages 90-92.

2 Complete steps 2-4 on page 61

3 Click where you want the first line segment to begin

Right-click if you want to draw with the background colour/style/

texture.

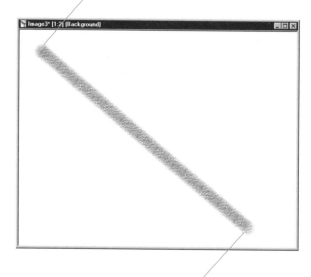

Repeat step 4 to define any further line segments which are

required.

4 Hold down Shift, then click where you want the first segment to end

Copying with the Clone brush

Cloning is the copying of colour from one location within an image to another (or to another image which has the same number of colours). To clone colours, you use the Clone brush.

Cloning

Refer to the Tool palette and do the following:

| Click here

Re step 4 – you should use the following notes as guidelines:

- *Shape – select a shape (e.g. Square or Horizontal)*

- *Size – select a brush size in pixels (in the range 1-255)*

- *Hardness – select a % in the range 0-100*

- *Opacity – select a % in the range 1-100 (100 = maximum opacity)*

- *Step (mimics brush contact) – select a % in the range 1-100*

- *Density – select a % in the range 1-100*

2 Refer to the Tool Options toolbar and do the following:

3 Ensure this tab is active

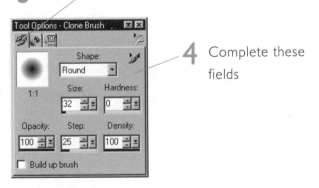

4 Complete these fields

5 Carry out the additional steps on page 64

6 Place the mouse pointer over the image section you want to copy

7 Right-click once

The Clone crosshairs indicate the pixel which is currently being copied.

As you drag in step 8, the crosshairs move, so you can select (on-the-fly) the area being copied.

8 Position the cursor where you want the paste operation to take place, then drag repeatedly

Magnified view of crosshairs

Replacing colours globally

You can have Paint Shop Pro replace a specified colour with another. You do this by nominating the colour you want to replace as the foreground colour, then selecting the new colour as the background colour. (Or vice versa).

You can replace colours:

- globally (within the whole of an image, or a selection area)

- manually (by using the Color Replacer tool as a brush)

Carrying out a global substitution

Refer to the Tool palette and do the following:

Click here

Re step 4 – you should use the following notes as guidelines:

- *Shape – select a shape (e.g. Square or Horizontal)*

- *Size – select a brush size in pixels (in the range 1-255)*

- *Step (mimics brush contact) – select a % in the range 1-100*

- *Density – select a % in the range 1-100*

2 Refer to the Tool Options toolbar and do the following:

3 Ensure this tab is active

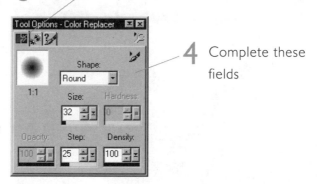

4 Complete these fields

5 Carry out the additional steps on page 66

6 Optional – if you want to limit the colour exchange to a selected area, define the relevant area now

7 Carry out step 8 OR 9 below:

8 Double-click the left mouse button to replace the background with the foreground colour

9 Double-click the right mouse button to replace the foreground with the background colour

The end result:

Here, the colour in the saucer has been replaced with white...

Replacing colours manually

Carrying out a manual substitution

Refer to the Tool palette and do the following:

Replacing colours manually requires a light touch (and experimentation with the available settings – see step 2).

| Click here

Re step 3 – you should carry out ONE of the following procedures:

- *drag with the left mouse button to replace the background with the foreground colour, or;*

- *drag with the right mouse button to replace the foreground with the background colour*

2 Complete steps 2-4 on page 65

3 Drag over the relevant area to carry out the substitution – see the DON'T FORGET tip

4 Release the mouse button when you've finished

Replacing colours with lines

Replacing colours with lines requires a light touch (and experimentation with the available settings).

The Color Replacer tool also lets you substitute colours as you create lines.

Replacing colours while drawing lines

Refer to the Tool palette and do the following:

Click here

Re steps 3-4 – you should carry out one of the following procedures:

- *click with the left mouse button to replace the background with the foreground colour, or;*

- *click with the right mouse button to replace the foreground with the background colour*

2 Complete steps 2-4 on page 65

3 Click where you want the line to start

Here, the roof is being replaced with white.

Repeat step 4 as often as necessary.

4 To create a line segment, hold down Shift and click elsewhere

Using the Dropper tool

You can activate the Dropper (within most paint tools) by holding down Ctrl.

The Dropper is an extremely useful tool which you can use to:

1. select a colour in the active image

2. nominate this as the active foreground or background colour

Using the Dropper

Refer to the Tool palette and do the following:

Re step 2 – you should carry out one of the following procedures:

- *click with the left mouse button to nominate the selected colour as the foreground, or;*

- *click with the right mouse button to nominate the selected colour as the background*

Click here

After step 2, the selected colour appears in the Color Palette:

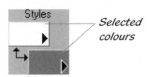
Selected colours

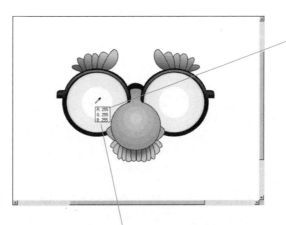

The makeup of the colour selected in step 2 displays in a fly-out:

R: 255
G: 255
B: 255

2 Click a colour – see the DON'T FORGET tip

Here, the fly-out indicates (using the RGB colour scheme) that the colour selected is white.

Retouching – an overview

You can use the Retouch tool to perform photo-retouching operations on images (or selected areas within images).

These operations include:

Lighten RGB	makes the image or selection brighter
Darken RGB	makes the image or selection darker
Soften	mutes the image or selection and diminishes contrast
Sharpen	emphasises edges and accentuates contrast
Emboss	produces a raised ('stamped') effect (where the foreground is emphasised in relation to the background)
Smudge	produces a stained, blurred effect
Push	like Smudge but no colour is picked up
Dodge	lightens image shadow
Burn	darkens images

All the above tools (excluding Dodge and Burn) work with images which are 24 bit (16 million colours) or greyscale; the remainder work only with 24 bit images.

Ways to use the Retouch tool

You can use the Retouch tool:

- as a brush

- to draw lines

Retouching images manually

Carrying out a manual retouch operation

Refer to the Tool palette and do the following:

Retouching images manually requires a light touch (and experimentation with the available settings – see step 2).

| Click here

After step 2, to select a retouch operation click this tab in the Tool Options toolbar:

Now click in the Retouch mode: field. In the list, select an operation.

For information on how to include patterns, textures or gradients in operations you perform with the Retouch tool, see page 33.

Here, an Emboss retouching operation is being carried out.

2 Complete steps 2-4 on page 65, as appropriate

3 Hold down the left mouse button and drag over the relevant area

4 Release the mouse button when you've finished

Retouching images with lines

To retouch images by defining lines, carry out the procedures described below.

Retouching images while drawing lines

Refer to the Tool palette and do the following:

Click here

Re step 4 – for how to complete these fields, see the HOT TIP on page 61.

2 Refer to the Tool Options toolbar and do the following:

3 Ensure this tab is active

After step 4, to select a retouch operation click this tab in the Tool Options toolbar:

Now click in the Retouch mode: field. In the list, select an operation.

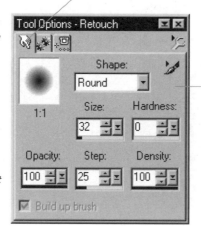

4 Complete these fields, as appropriate

5 Click where you want the retouch operation to begin

For information on how to include patterns, textures or gradients in operations you perform with the Retouch tool, see page 33.

Here, a Burn retouching operation is being carried out.

Repeat step 6 for as many extra line segments as you want to insert.

6 Hold down Shift and click where you want the line segment to end

Painting with the Airbrush

You can use the Airbrush tool to simulate painting with a spray can. You can do this in two ways:

- while using the Airbrush as a brush

- while using the Airbrush to draw lines

Using the Airbrush as a brush

Refer to the Tool palette and do the following:

Click here

You can also select and apply a brush type.
After step 3, click this button on the right of the Tool Options toolbar:

In the menu, select a brush (e.g. Paintbrush or Charcoal).
(Alternatively, click Custom in the menu. In the Custom Brush dialog, click a brush. Finally, click OK.)

2 Refer to the Tool Options toolbar and do the following:

3 Ensure this tab is active

4 Complete these fields, as appropriate (see the HOT TIP on page 61)

...cont'd

5 Carry out step 6 OR 7 below:

6 Hold down the left mouse button, then drag to paint with the active foreground colour/style/texture

Here, the Shape setting (see step 4 on the facing page) has been set to Left Slash.

For information on how to include patterns, textures or gradients in operations you perform with the Airbrush tool, see page 33.

7 Hold down the right mouse button, then drag to paint with the active background colour/style/texture

8 Release the mouse button

Drawing with the Airbrush

Using the Airbrush to draw lines
Refer to the Tool palette and do the following:

You can also select and apply a brush type.
After step 3, click this button on the right of the Tool Options toolbar:

In the menu, select a brush (e.g. Paintbrush or Charcoal).
(Alternatively, click Custom in the menu. In the Custom Brush dialog, click a brush. Finally, click OK.)

Click here

2 Refer to the Tool Options toolbar and do the following:

3 Ensure this tab is active

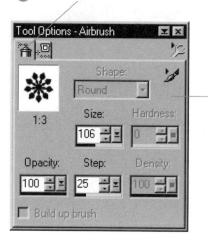

4 Complete these fields, as appropriate (see the HOT TIP on page 61)

...cont'd

5 Click where you want the
retouch operation to begin

*For information
on how to
include
patterns,
textures or
gradients in operations you
perform with the Airbrush
tool, see page 33.*

*Here, a custom
brush has been
applied – see
the HOT TIP on
the facing page.*

*Repeat step 6
for as many
extra line
segments as
you want to
insert.*

6 Hold down Shift and click where
you want the line segment to end

3. Painting and drawing | 77

Inserting colours with the Fill tool

You can use the Fill tool to

- fill an image with colour

- fill an image with a specific image you've already opened into an additional window

- fill an image with a gradient (Paint Shop Pro supports 4 kinds: Linear, Rectangular, Sunburst, Radial)

Filling images with a colour

Refer to the Tool palette and do the following:

If you want to limit the fill to a selection area, define it before step 1.

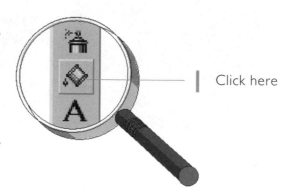

Click here

Re step 4 – you should use the following notes as guidelines:

- *Blend mode – all options except Normal ensure that the fill is affected by the underlying image colours*

- *Match mode – select the method by which Paint Shop Pro decides which pixels are covered (None covers all pixels)*

- *Opacity – select a % in the range 1-100 (100 is maximum opacity), and;*

- *Tolerance – enter a value in this range: 0 (only exact matches are filled) to 200 (every pixel is filled)*

2 Refer to the Tool Options toolbar and do the following:

3 Ensure this tab is active

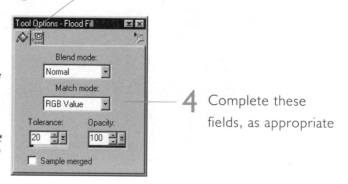

4 Complete these fields, as appropriate

5 Left-click to insert the foreground
colour, OR right-click to insert the
background colour

*For information
on how to
include
patterns,
textures or
gradients in operations you
perform with the Fill tool,
see page 33.*

A completed colour fill:

Inserting images as patterns

You can use the Colour Palette to apply images as patterns to other images.

Filling an image with another

First, open:

1. the image you want to insert

2. the image into which you want to insert it

Now refer to the Colour Palette and do the following:

To insert a preset pattern into images as a foreground fill, follow steps 1-4. In step 5, however, select a pre-defined pattern. (To insert a preset pattern as a background fill, note that steps 1-3 should refer to the lower Styles button.) Finally, carry out step 6.

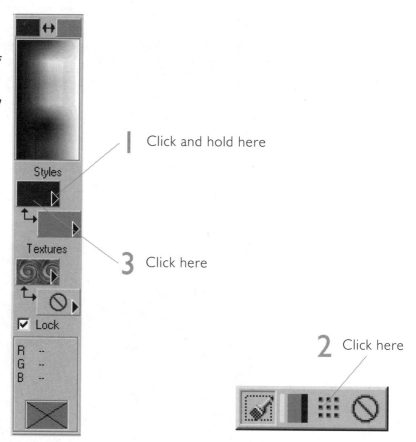

Click and hold here

3 Click here

2 Click here

4 Click here

Note that the images you apply pattern fills to must be at least:

• *24 bit (16 million colours), or;*

• *greyscale*

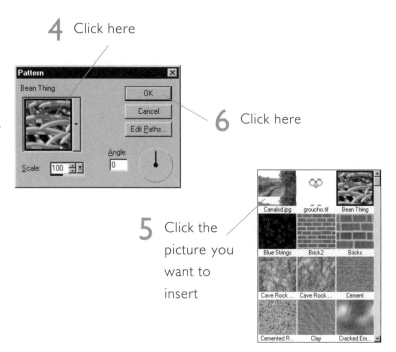

6 Click here

5 Click the picture you want to insert

6 Follow steps 1-4 on page 78, then left-click in the host image to insert the picture/pattern

Two images combined in an unusual way:

Inserting gradients

The procedures described here insert a gradient in the foreground. To insert one as a background fill, note that steps 1 and 3 should refer to the lower Styles button...

You can use the Colour Palette to apply gradients to images.

Filling images with a gradient

First, open the image you want to fill (or pre-define a selection area). Now refer to the Colour Palette and do the following:

Note that you can choose from the following non-linear gradient types:

Rectangular

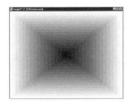

Sunburst

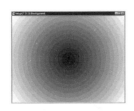

Radial

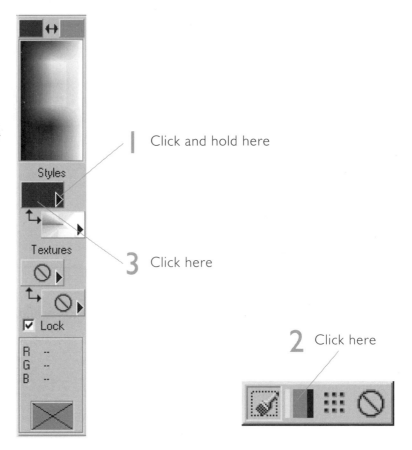

Click and hold here

3 Click here

2 Click here

...cont'd

 Before you carry out step 6, select a gradient type here:

The topmost icon creates a linear gradient. For details of the other icons, see the HOT TIP on the facing page.

 Note that the images you apply gradients to must be at least:

• *24 bit (16 million colours), or;*

• *greyscale*

 Additional tools with which you can apply gradients include the following:

• *Paintbrush*
• *Clone*
• *Colour Replacer*
• *Retouch*
• *Airbrush*

4 Click here

6 Click here

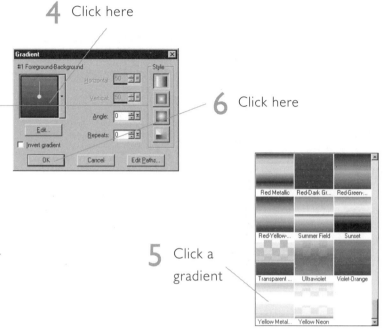

5 Click a gradient

7 Follow steps 1-4 on page 78, then left-click in the image to insert the gradient

A radial gradient applied to a bitmap:

Inserting textures

You can use the Colour Palette to apply gradients to images.

Filling images with a texture

First, open the image you want to fill (or pre-define a selection area). Now refer to the Colour Palette and do the following:

The procedures described here insert a texture in the foreground. To insert one as a background fill, note that steps 1 and 3 should refer to the lower Textures button...

You can only apply textures in conjunction with active foreground or background styles.

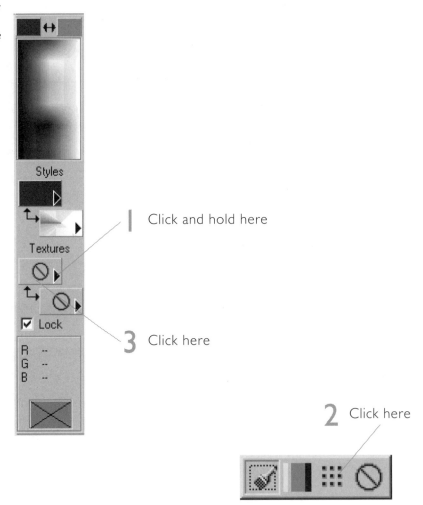

Click and hold here

Click here

Click here

...cont'd

4 Click here

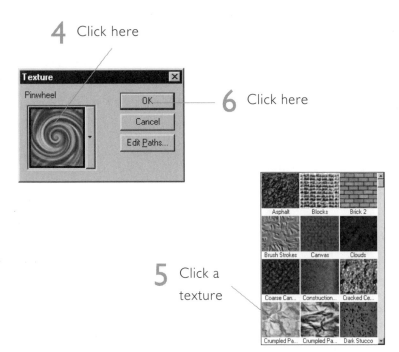

6 Click here

Note that the images you apply textures to must be at least:

- *24 bit (16 million colours), or;*
- *greyscale*

5 Click a texture

7 Follow steps 1-4 on page 78, then left-click in the image to insert the gradient

Additional tools with which you can apply gradients include the following:

- *Paintbrush*
- *Clone*
- *Colour Replacer*
- *Retouch*
- *Airbrush*

A texture applied to a bitmap:

Inserting text with the Text tool

Paint Shop Pro lets you insert text into images, easily and conveniently. You can insert two principal types of text:

You can also create Selection (raster) text. Selection text is an empty, transparent selection e.g.:

Once created, Selection text can be edited with Paint Shop Pro's tools. In the following example, a different gradient fill has been applied to each letter:

Floating	Floating text appears above the current layer
Vector	You can only create vector text on a vector layer. Vector text is actually a vector object; as a result, it can be edited, moved and deformed. (It can also be added to paths.)

When you create text, you can specify:

1.   a typeface and/or type size

2.   a style. With most typefaces, you can choose from:

    –   Regular

    –   *Italic*

    –   Bold

3.   the following text effects

    –   ~~Strikethrough~~

    –   <u>Underline</u>

4.   an alignment. You can choose from:

    –   Left

    –   Center

    –   Right

Anti-aliasing is the process of removing jagged distortions; it makes text look and print smoother.

You can also elect to have Paint Shop Pro 'anti-alias' the text.

You can insert vector text onto simple vector object outlines. With the Text tool active in the Tool palette, move the mouse pointer over the relevant vector object until the cursor changes:

The new cursor

Now click the vector object. Complete the Text Entry dialog in line with steps 4-9 on page 88 (ensure Vector is selected in step 6, and make sure you select the appropriate alignment in step 7).

Aligned text

Inserting text

Refer to the Tool palette and do the following:

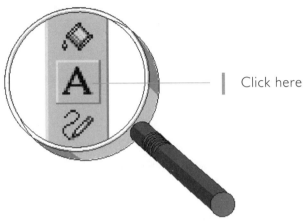

| Click here

2 Place the mouse pointer where you want the text inserted

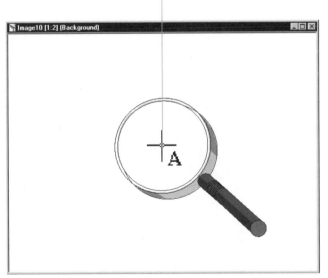

3 Left-click once

...cont'd

You can insert vector text onto open vector paths (open paths have start and end points).

With the Text tool active in the Tool palette, move the mouse pointer over the relevant vector path until the cursor changes:

The new cursor

Now click the path. Complete the Text Entry dialog in line with steps 4-9 (ensure Vector is selected in step 6, and make sure you select the appropriate alignment in step 7).

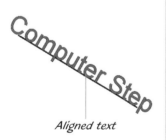

Aligned text

4 Click here; in the list, select a font

5 Click here; in the list, select a type size

7 Click I or more formatting options

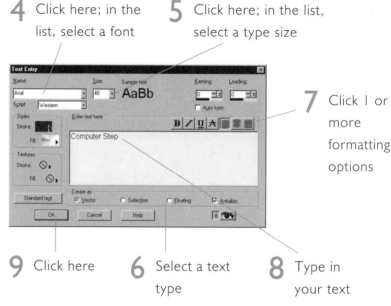

9 Click here

6 Select a text type

8 Type in your text

Text in action:

Editing text

Paint Shop Pro lets you edit inserted vector text. Do the following:

You can only edit raster text in a limited way. For instance, you

can:

* *apply fills with the paint tools, or;*
* *cut or delete non-floating text*

using standard selection editing techniques.

| Click here in
the Tool palette

You can also use the Layer palette to access the Text Entry dialog.
If the Layer palette isn't on-screen, right-click any toolbar and select Layer Palette. Do the following:

Find – then double-click – the Text layer

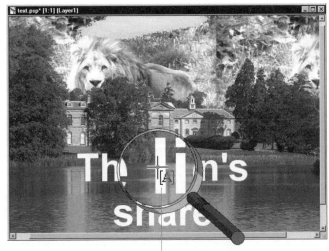

2 Place the mouse pointer over the text and left-click – the Text Entry dialog launches

3 Carry out steps 4-7 (as appropriate) on the facing page

4 Carry out step 8 on the facing page (but amend the existing text as appropriate)

5 Carry out step 9 on the facing page

Drawing with the Draw tool

After step 1, click this tab in the Tool Options toolbar:

Now click in the Type: field. In the list, select Single Line. Also, click in the Line style: field and select a style in the list – e.g., you can select a dotted line, or one with arrowheads on one or both ends.

Finally, enter a line width in the Width: field (in the range 1-255) and select Create as vector (for a fully editable line).

Paint Shop Pro has a separate tool which you can use to create more detailed lines/curves.

You can draw:

- Single lines

- Freehand lines

- Bezier curves

You can create lines/curves as rasters or vectors (vectors are much more editable).

Drawing single lines

Refer to the Tool palette and do the following:

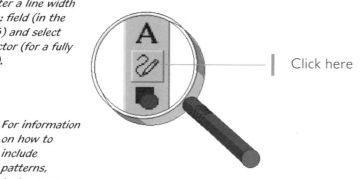

Click here

For information on how to include patterns, textures or gradients in operations you perform with the Draw tool, see page 33.

2 Place the mouse pointer where you want the line to start

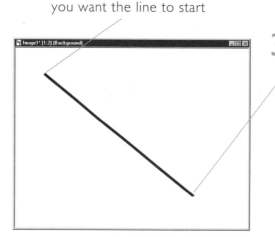

3 Drag with the left mouse button to draw the line

Drawing single lines with multiple segments

Refer to the Tool palette and do the following:

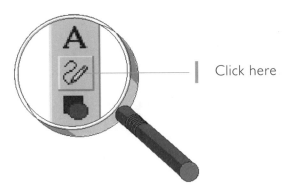

| Click here

2 Place the mouse pointer where you want the line to start, then left-click once

3 Hold down Alt

4 Click where you want the segment to end, and click again

5 Repeat for as many segments as you want to add, still holding down Alt

After step 6, Paint Shop Pro fills out the line outline.

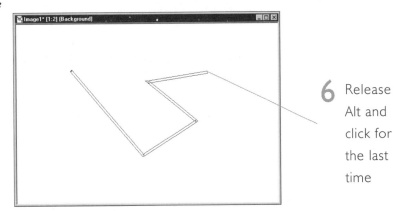

6 Release Alt and click for the last time

Drawing Freehand lines

Refer to the Tool palette and do the following:

| Click here

For information on how to include patterns, textures or gradients in operations you perform with the Draw tool, see page 33.

2 Refer to the Tool Options toolbar and do the following:

3 Ensure this tab is active

Select Create as vector to define a vector Freehand line, or deselect this to create a raster line.

4 Click here; in the list, select Freehand Line

5 Complete the remaining fields, as appropriate

Here, a vector Freehand line has been defined.

After step 6, release the mouse button.

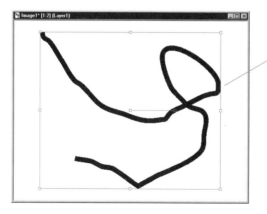

6 Drag with the left mouse button to draw with the foreground colour, or with the right to draw with the background colour

...cont'd

Drawing Bezier curves

Refer to the Tool palette and do the following:

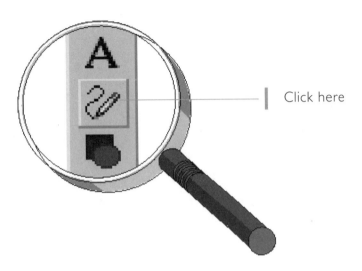

Click here

2 Refer to the Tool Options toolbar and do the following:

3 Ensure this tab is active

Select Create as vector to define a vector Freehand line, or deselect this to create a raster line.

4 Click here; in the list, select Bezier Curve

5 Complete the remaining fields, as appropriate

6 Carry out the additional steps on page 94

HOT TIP

7 Place the mouse pointer where you want the curve to start

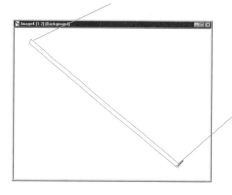

8 Drag with the left mouse button to define the curve's length

9 Click away from the start point to set the start target angle

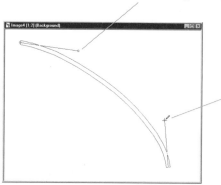

10 Click away from the end point to set the end target angle

The end result:

Here, a raster curve has been defined.

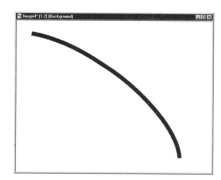

Using the Picture Tube tool

You can also paint using object collections called 'picture tubes'. When you do this, Paint Shop Pro automatically inserts a variety of related objects. For instance, if you paint with the Fish picture tube, a dozen different fish types are inserted...

Painting with the Picture Tube tool

Refer to the Tool palette and do the following:

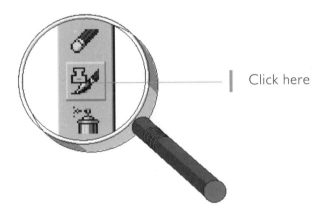

Click here

2 Refer to the Tool Options toolbar and do the following:

Re step 5 – complete the fields in line with the following guidelines:

- *Scale – set the tube size (in the range 10%-250%)*

- *Step – increase the step setting to give less contact between the brush tip and the image surface. The result is that the tube's outline is more prominent, and the stroke less dense*

3 Ensure this tab is active

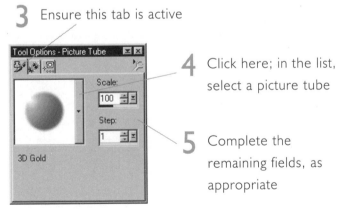

4 Click here; in the list, select a picture tube

5 Complete the remaining fields, as appropriate

6 Carry out the additional steps on pages 96-97

7 Ensure this tab is active

Re step 8 –
complete the
fields in line
with the
following
guidelines:

- Placement mode – select
Random (objects appear
at random intervals) or
Continuous (objects are
inserted at equal
intervals), and;

- Selection mode – select
Random (objects are
chosen haphazardly);
Incremental (objects are
inserted one at a time);
Angular (objects appear
according to painting
direction); or Velocity
(objects appear according
to painting speed)

8 Select values in
these fields

9 Optional – click here for advanced
options, then follow steps 10-11

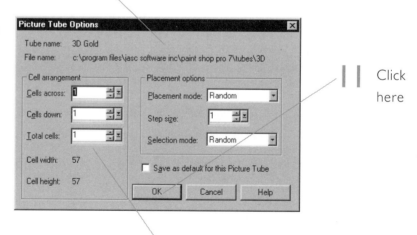

11 Click
here

10 Customise cell arrangement
details (but note the effect can
sometimes be undesirable)

12 Place the mouse pointer where you want the tube to start

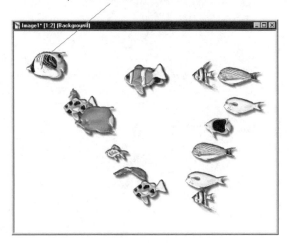

13 Drag with the left mouse button, then release it

Another picture tube:

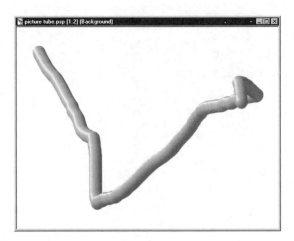

The 3D Gold picture tube

Drawing with the Preset Shapes tool

You can create shapes (e.g. arrows, circles and stars, or more complex vectors).

Using the Preset Shapes tool
Refer to the Tool palette and do the following:

| Click here

2 Refer to the Tool Options toolbar and do the following:

Select Create as vector to define a vector shape, or deselect this to create a raster one.

3 Ensure this tab is active

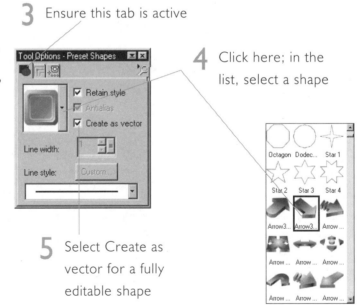

4 Click here; in the list, select a shape

5 Select Create as vector for a fully editable shape

6 Drag with the left mouse button to draw the shape

When you've created a vector shape, you can save it to your own library for future use.

With the vector open, pull down the File menu and click Export, Shape. In the Export Shape Library dialog, name the vector. Click OK.

(To use the new shape, follow steps 1-6.)

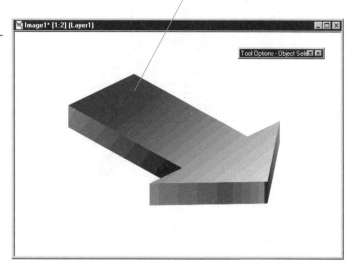

Another Preset shape:

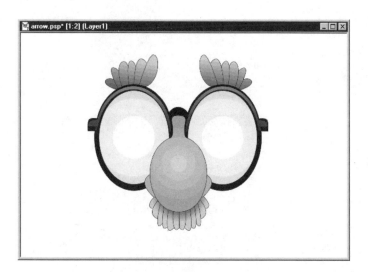

Editing Preset shapes

To edit vector shapes/objects:

1 Refer to the Tool palette and do the following:

2 Click here

You can apply a new fill to vectors. Click the Styles/Fill box then do the following:

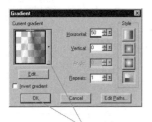

Click here. Select a new fill in the list, then click OK

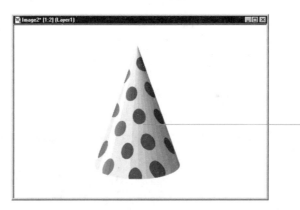

3 Double-click the vector

A new fill has been applied

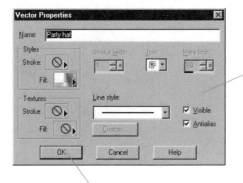

4 Complete the dialog (e.g. to amend the shape width, enter a new entry in the Stroke width field)

Re step 4 – depending on the vector selected, some of the options may be greyed out and therefore unavailable.

5 Click here

Node editing – an overview

Vector objects consist of a path with at least one contour. The more complex the vector, the more contours it has. Contours, in turn, consist of:

• two or more nodes (control points)

• linking segments (straight or curved)

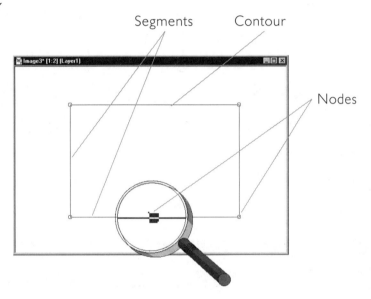

Editing (manipulating) nodes is carried out in a special mode called Node Edit. Node Edit mode:

• displays the vector's path

• does not accurately reflect the vector's true appearance

Only one path can be edited at once, but you can use nodes to reshape vector objects in an almost infinite number of ways.

Launching Node Edit mode

To enter Node Edit mode (preparatory to manipulating vector nodes), do the following:

1 Activate this button in the Tool palette:

2 Right-click the vector object you want to edit; in the menu, select Node Edit

To leave Node Edit mode, perform one of the following operations:

- *to leave Node Edit without applying any changes you've made, press Esc*

- *to leave Node Edit and apply any changes you've made, press Ctrl+Q. (Alternatively, right-click the vector and choose Quit Node Editing from the menu.)*

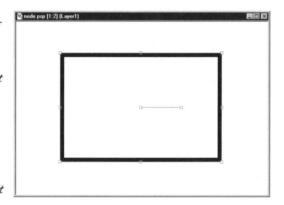

A selected vector object in normal mode

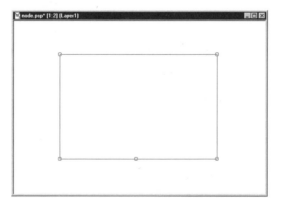

The same vector object in Node Edit mode

Node operations

You can create a new contour by adding a new node.

In Node Edit mode, press Ctrl+E. Left-click away from a segment. Now either:

You can create a new contour by adding a new node.

In Node Edit mode, press Ctrl+E. Left-click away from a segment. Now either:

- *Left-click once to create a straight segment, or;*
- *Drag with the mouse to create a curved segment*

Adding new nodes

In Node Edit mode, do the following:

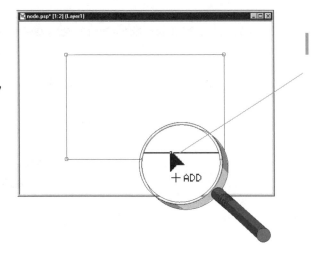

Hold down Ctrl (the mouse pointer changes) as you left-click a contour

Moving nodes

In Node Edit mode, do the following:

Drag a marquee around 1 or more nodes to select them

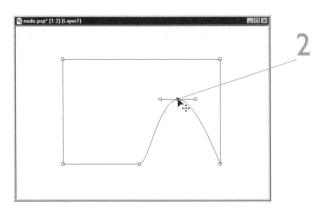

Drag the node(s) to a new location (thus warping the vector)

You can also select multiple nodes by holding down Shift as you click them.

Dragging a segment rather than a node moves the entire contour.

If you've only selected one node, you can move it in increments of 45°. Simply hold down Shift as you drag.

Changing a node's type

Applying a new type to a node has an impact on the segments which enter and leave it.

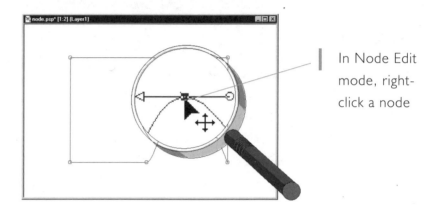

In Node Edit mode, right-click a node

2 In the menu, click Node Type. In the sub-menu, select a node type

Merging nodes

When you 'merge' a node, you delete it. This results in the two segments which enter it being united into one.

Follow step 1 above to select a node, then press Ctrl+M

You can merge multiple nodes. However, note the following caveats:

- *the effect can be hard to predict*
- *merging every node within a contour deletes the contour*

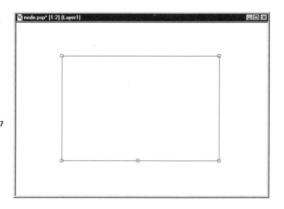

The illustration at the base of page 103, after the node flagged by step 2 has been merged

Breaking nodes

You can 'break' nodes. This means that the contour in which the node is situated is:

- split into two separate contours (if the original contour was open)

- opened out (if the original contour was closed)

To join nodes (contours), hold down Ctrl as you drag one node over another. When the pointer looks like this:

JOIN

release the mouse button.

Left-click a node

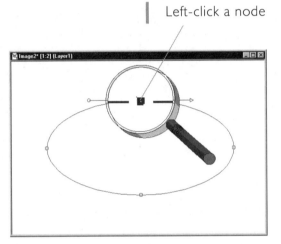

To copy a contour, select the relevant nodes then press Ctrl+C. To paste in the contour, press Ctrl+V. (The new contour is inserted with a slight offset.)

2 Press Ctrl +K , then drag the nodes apart

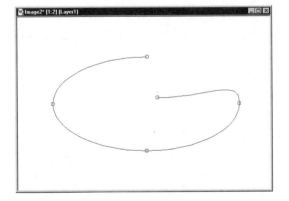

Here, the closed ellipse in the upper illustration has been opened

Using node handles

Two handles extend from every node. You can use these to redefine the shape of the host contour.

Node handles vary according to the node type. For instance, Cusp node handles move independently...

Handles

Control handles

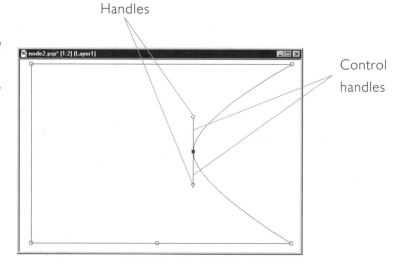

Hold down Shift to constrain the reshaping to 45° increments.

Drag a handle to a new location to reshape the contour

Here, the fact that the node is Symmetrical has ensured that the upper handle has also moved an equal distance i.e. the control handles are equal in length. (With Asymmetrical nodes, the handles can vary in size.)

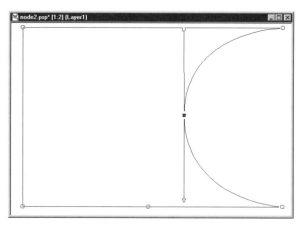

The bottom handle has been dragged straight down

Using filters

In this chapter, you'll learn how to add a variety of creative effects to images (or image selections). You'll do this by applying any of Paint Shop Pro's numerous filters. Finally, you'll create your own filters; amend user-defined filters; and apply these to images or image selections.

Covers

Chapter Four

Using the Edge Enhance filter

Filters are distinct from deformations and effects because they vary the colour of every pixel (picture element) in line with:

- *its current colour*

- *the colours of any neighbouring pixels*

If you only want to apply these filters to a part of the image, define the appropriate selection area first.

Applying Edge Enhance

Pull down the Effects menu and click Effect Browser. Now do the following:

Click Edge Enhance

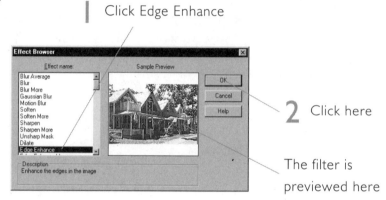

2 Click here

The filter is previewed here

Edge Enhance in action:

Use the Edge Enhance filter (it works by amplifying edge contrast) to increase image clarity.

Re step 1 – to apply the Edge Enhance More filter instead (for an enhanced effect), select Edge Enhance More.

You can also use a menu route to apply this filter. Pull down the Effects menu and click Edge, Enhance.

Before applying the filter

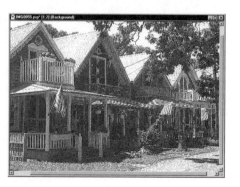

After applying the filter

Using the Find Edges filter

Use the Find Edges filter (it works by darkening an image and emphasising its edges) to increase image clarity.

Note that filters only work with the following image types:

- *coloured images with more than 256 colours, and;*
- *256-colour greyscales*

Applying Find Edges

Pull down the Effects menu and click Effect Browser. Now do the following:

Click Find Edges

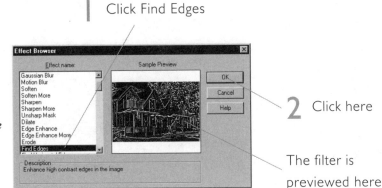

2 Click here

The filter is previewed here

Find Edges in action:

If the image you want to apply a filter to doesn't meet the criteria in the BEWARE tip, press Ctrl+Shift+0 (zero) to increase the colour depth to 16 million.

(If this produces undesirable effects, try applying the Average filter – see page 122.)

Before applying the filter

After applying the filter

You can also use a menu route to apply this filter. Pull down the Effects menu and click Edge, Find All.

Using the Horizontal Edges filter

If you only want to apply the filter to a part of the image, define the appropriate selection area first.

Use the Find Horizontal Edges filter (it works by darkening an image and then emphasising its horizontal edges) when you need to identify – and emphasise – those parts of an image which have significant horizontal colour transitions.

Applying Horizontal Edges

Pull down the Effects menu and click Effect Browser. Now do the following:

Click Find Horizontal Edges

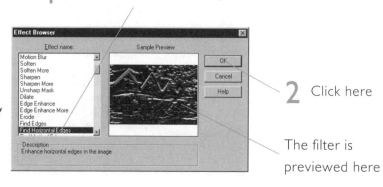

2 Click here

The filter is previewed here

Horizontal Edges in action:

Experiment with applying more than one filter to images (or the same filter more than once) – the effects can be dramatic.

You can also use a menu route to apply this filter. Pull down the Effects menu and click Edge, Find Horizontal.

Before applying the filter

After applying the filter

Using the Vertical Edges filter

If you only want to apply the filter to a part of the image, define the appropriate selection area first.

The Find Vertical Edges filter works by darkening an image and then emphasising its vertical edges.

Re step 1 – to apply the Edge Enhance More filter instead (for an enhanced effect), select Edge Enhance More.

You can also use a menu route to apply this filter. Pull down the Effects menu and click Edge, Find Vertical.

Applying Vertical Edges

Pull down the Effects menu and click Effect Browser. Now do the following:

Click Find Vertical Edges

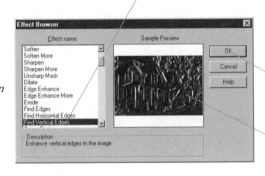

2 Click here

The filter is previewed here

Vertical Edges in action:

Before applying the filter

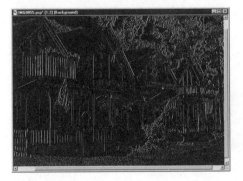

After applying the filter

Using the Trace Contour filter

If you only want to apply the filter to a part of the image, define the appropriate selection area first.

Applying Trace Contour

Pull down the Effects menu and click Effect Browser. Now do the following:

Click Trace Contour

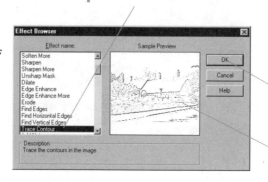

The Trace Contour filter is a specialist edge filter which, effectively, outlines images by defining a border around them.

2 Click here

The filter is previewed here

Paint Shop Pro offers more specialist filters. For example, use the Deinterlace filter to correct video images.

Ensure no selection area has been defined. Pull down the Effects menu and click Enhance Photo, Deinterlace. Complete the dialog, then click OK.

Trace Contour in action:

Before applying the filter

You can also use a menu route to apply this filter. Pull down the Effects menu and click Edge, Trace Contour.

After applying the filter

Using the Edge Preserving filter

If you only want to apply the filter to a part of the image, define a selection area first.

Applying Edge Preserving

Pull down the Effects menu and click Effect Browser. In the left column in the Browser, double-click Edge Preserving Smooth. Do the following:

This filter removes noise without loss of edge detail.

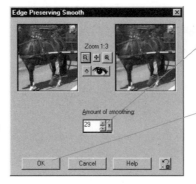

Re step 1 – the permitted range is 1-30.

1 Specify a smoothing figure

2 Click OK

Edge Preserving in action:

You can also use a menu to apply this filter. Pull down the Effects menu and click Noise, Edge Preserving Smooth. Now complete the dialog in line with steps 1-2.

Before applying the filter

After applying the filter (its impact has been emphasised for effect)

Using the Blur filter

If you only want to apply the filter to a part of the image, define a selection area first.

The Blur filter lightens pixels which adjoin the hard edges of defined lines and shaded areas, making for a hazy effect.

Re step 1 – to apply the Blur More filter instead (for enhanced effect), select Blur More.

Use these additional filters to achieve blur variations:

- *Motion Blur — adds direction to the blur, or;*
- *Gaussian Blur — blurs pixels incrementally*

To apply either of these, pull down the Effects menu and select Blur. Now click Gaussian Blur or Motion Blur. Complete the dialog then click OK.

You can also use a menu to apply this filter. Pull down the Effects menu and click Blur, Blur.

Applying Blur

Pull down the Effects menu and click Effect Browser. Now do the following:

 Click Blur

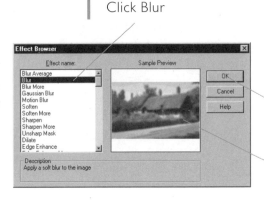

2 Click here

The filter is previewed here

Blur in action:

Before applying the filter

After applying the filter

Using the Soften filter

If you only want to apply the filter to a part of the image, define a selection area first.

The Soften filter diminishes image graininess.
By applying this filter more than once, you can simulate the effect of motion.

Applying Soften

Pull down the Effects menu and click Effect Browser. Now do the following:

Click Soften

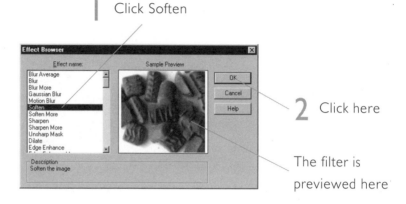

2 Click here

The filter is previewed here

Re step 1 – to apply the Soften More filter instead (for enhanced effect), select Soften More.

Soften in action:

Before applying the filter

You can also use a menu to apply this filter. Pull down the Effects menu and click Blur, Soften.

After applying the filter (its impact has been emphasised for effect)

Using the Sharpen filter

If you only want to apply the filter to a part of the image, define a selection area first.

The Sharpen filter improves an image's focus and clarity.

Re step 2 – to apply the Sharpen More filter instead (for enhanced effect), select Sharpen More.

Applying Sharpen

Pull down the Effects menu and click Effect Browser. Now do the following:

Click Sharpen

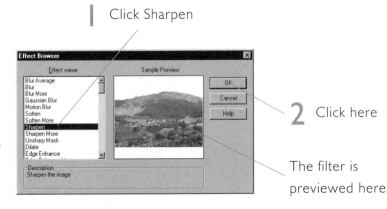

2 Click here

The filter is previewed here

Sharpen in action:

You can also sharpen images (though in a different way) by using the paradoxically named Unsharpen filter.

Pull down the Effects menu and click Sharpen, Unsharp Mask. In the Unsharp Mask dialog, adjust the settings in the Radius, Clipping and Strength fields appropriately.

Finally, click OK.

Before applying the filter

You can also use a menu route to apply the Sharpen filter. Pull down the Effects menu and click Sharpen, Sharpen.

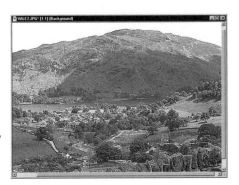

After applying the filter (its impact has been emphasised for effect)

Using the Add Noise filter

If you only want to apply the filter to a part of the image, define a selection area first.

The Add Noise filter ensures that images have randomly distributed colour pixels; you can determine, in a special dialog, the extent and type of the distribution.

Re step 1 – the permitted range is 1 (almost no noise) to 100 (maximum noise).

Re step 2 – choose Uniform for an effect which more closely resembles the original image.

You can also use a menu to apply this filter. Pull down the Effects menu and click Noise, Add. Now complete the dialog in line with steps 1-3.

Applying Add Noise

Pull down the Effects menu and click Effect Browser. In the left column in the Browser, double-click Add Noise. Do the following:

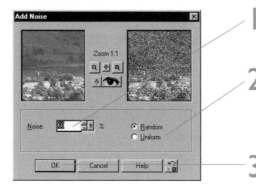

1 Specify the noise required

2 Select a distribution method

3 Click OK

Add Noise in action:

Before applying the filter

After applying the filter

Using the Despeckle filter

If you only want to apply the filter to a part of the image, define a selection area first.

The Despeckle blurs all of an image except those locations (edges) where meaningful colour changes take place.

You can sometimes use Despeckle to remove small scratches in images.

Applying Despeckle

Pull down the Effects menu and click Effect Browser. Now do the following:

Click Despeckle

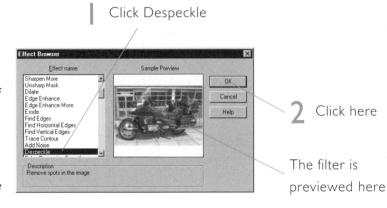

2 Click here

The filter is previewed here

Despeckle in action:

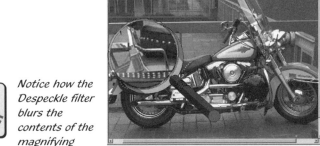

Before applying the filter

Notice how the Despeckle filter blurs the contents of the magnifying lens.

You can also use a menu to apply this filter. Pull down the Effects menu and click Noise, Despeckle. Now complete the dialog in line with steps 1-2.

After applying the filter

Using the Dilate filter

If you only want to apply the filter to a part of the image, define a selection area first.

The Dilate filter enhances light areas in an image.

You can also use a menu to apply this filter. Pull down the Effects menu and click Edge, Dilate.

Applying Dilate

Pull down the Effects menu and click Effect Browser. Now do the following:

1 Click Dilate

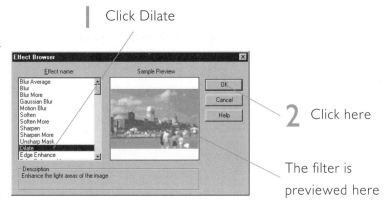

2 Click here

The filter is previewed here

Dilate in action:

Before applying the filter

After applying the filter (its impact has been emphasised for effect)

Using the Median filter

If you only want to apply the filter to a part of the image, define a selection area first.

The Median filter reduces image noise by 'averaging' pixel brightness and discarding pixels which have relatively little in common with their neighbours.

Re step 1 – the permitted range is 3-31.

Applying Median

Pull down the Effects menu and click Effect Browser. In the left column in the Browser, double-click Median Filter. Do the following:

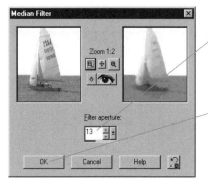

1   Specify a filter aperture

2   Click OK

Median in action:

You can also use a menu to apply this filter. Pull down the Effects menu and click Noise, Median Filter. Now complete the dialog in line with steps 1-2.

Before applying the filter

After applying the filter

Using the Texture Preserving filter

If you only want to apply the filter to a part of the image, define a selection area first.

Applying Texture Preserving

Pull down the Effects menu and click Effect Browser. In the left column in the Browser, double-click Texture Preserving Smooth. Do the following:

This filter removes noise without loss of texture detail.

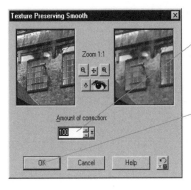

I Specify a smoothing figure

2 Click OK

Re step 1 – the permitted range is 1-30.

Texture Preserving in action:

You can also use a menu to apply this filter. Pull down the Effects menu and click Noise, Texture Preserving Smooth. Now complete the dialog in line with steps 1-2.

Before applying the filter

After applying the filter

Using the Average filter

If you only want to apply the filter to a part of the image, define a selection area first.

Applying Average

Pull down the Effects menu and click Effect Browser. In the left column in the Browser, double-click Blur Average. Do the following:

This filter removes noise which is spread over the whole of an image.

(You can also use it when increasing an image's colour depth to 16 million colours produces an unwelcome 'dithering' effect.)

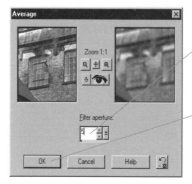

I Specify an aperture setting

2 Click OK

Re step 1 – the permitted range is 3-31.

Average in action:

You can also use a menu to apply this filter. Pull down the Effects menu and click Blur, Average. Now complete the dialog in line with steps 1-2.

1 – an image with added noise

2 – the filter has removed much of the noise

Using the Salt and Pepper filter

This filter removes noise/ specks (e.g. dust) from photographs. It works best when you apply it to a pre-defined selection.

You can also use a menu to apply this filter. Pull down the Effects menu and click Noise, Salt and Pepper filter. Now complete the dialog in line with steps 1-2.

Applying Salt and Pepper

Pull down the Effects menu and click Effect Browser. In the left column in the Browser, double-click Salt & Pepper Filter. Do the following:

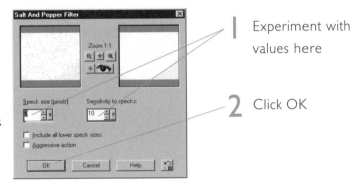

1 Experiment with values here

2 Click OK

Salt and Pepper in action:

This is illustration 1 on the facing page – Salt and Pepper has cleared the noise in the selection area

You can remove moiré from scanned photographs.

An example of moiré (technically, the superimposition of two geometrical patterns, such as grids)

Pull down the Effects menu and click Enhance Photo, Moiré Pattern Removal. Complete the dialog, then click OK.

User-defined filters

You can define your own filters, easily and conveniently. Once created, new filters can be named, saved and applied to images whenever required.

The next illustration shows an image before the application of a user-defined filter:

Applying this user-defined filter has arguably improved the image: the sky looks better.

Paint Shop Pro provides some further examples of customised filters.

Press F1 to launch HELP. Click Help Topics. Click this tab:

Search for 'Example Filters'.

And now the result of applying the filter:

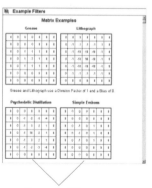

Sample filters

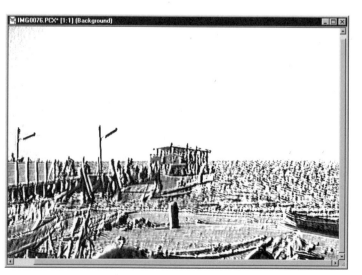

Creating filters

Defining your own filter

Pull down the Effects menu and click User Defined. Now carry out the following steps:

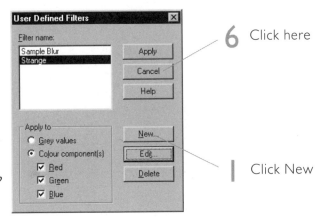

6 Click here

1 Click New

Slight amendments to any values in the Filter matrix can produce a marked effect.

For instance, changing the final value (-7) to -9 makes the image look like this:

The settings shown in the matrix on the right produce the effect demonstrated on the facing page.

2 Name the new filter

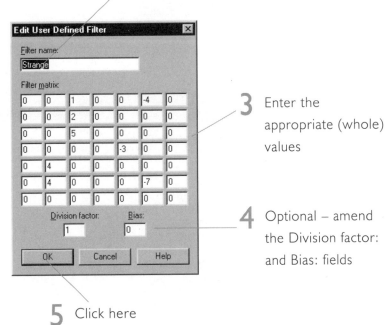

3 Enter the appropriate (whole) values

4 Optional – amend the Division factor: and Bias: fields

5 Click here

Applying user-defined filters

1 Open the image you want to apply the filter to

2 Optional – to limit the effect of the filter, define the relevant selection area

3 Pull down the Effects menu and carry out these steps:

To edit an existing user-defined filter, follow steps 1-5 on the right. Omit step 6. Instead, click this button:

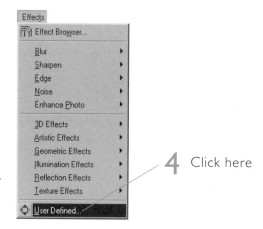

4 Click here

5 Select a filter

In the Edit User Defined Filter dialog, make the relevant adjustments in line with steps 3-4 on page 125. Click OK.

Finally, click Cancel. (Alternatively, follow step 6 to apply the amended filter immediately.)

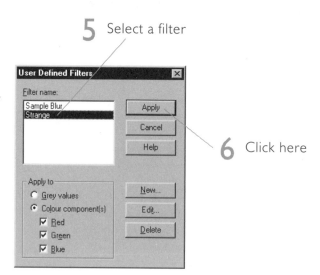

6 Click here

Using deformations

In this chapter, you'll add additional creative effects to images (or image selections) by applying specialist deformations.

Covers

Chapter Five

The Circle deformation

In Paint Shop Pro, deformations are distinct from filters and effects in that they work by transferring data from one image area to another.

The Circle deformation produces a 'fish-eye' effect.

After Circle has been applied

For how to use masks, see chapter 7.

To apply this deformation via a menu route, ignore steps 2-4. Instead, pull down the Effects menu and select Geometric Effects, Circle.

Applying the Circle deformation

1 Optional – to limit the deformation to part of the image, define the relevant selection area or mask

2 Pull down the Effects menu and select Effect Browser

Experiment with applying more than one deformation to images (or the same deformation more than once) – the results can be dramatic.

3 Click Circle

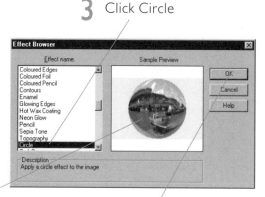

The result of applying the chosen deformation is previewed here:

4 Click here

The CurlyQs deformation

Note that images must fall into the following categories:

- coloured images with more than 256 colours
- 256-colour greyscales

for deformations to work on them.

(If the image you want to apply a deformation to doesn't meet these criteria, carry out the procedure in the HOT TIP on page 109.)

The CurlyQs deformation splits images into curled columns.

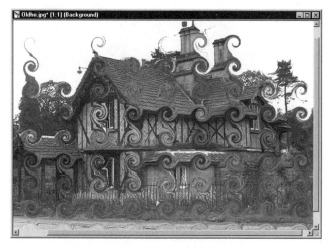

After CurlyQ has been applied

If you want to limit the deformation to a selection area or mask, define it before step 1.

Applying the CurlyQs deformation

1 Pull down the Effects menu and select Effect Browser

To apply this deformation via a menu route, ignore steps 1-2. Instead, pull down the Effects menu and select Geometric Effects, CurlyQs. Now complete steps 3-5.

2 In the leftmost column in the Browser, select CurlyQs then click OK

3 Specify the no. of columns/rows

You can also specify the deformation direction. Choose:

- Clockwise, or;
- CounterClockwise.

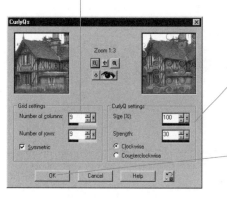

4 Specify the CurlyQ size and strength

5 Click here

The Cylinder deformations

If you only want to apply the deformation to a part of the image, define a selection area first.

Of the two cylinder deformations, the Cylinder - Horizontal deformation stretches an image horizontally, while the Cylinder - Vertical deformation stretches it vertically.

You can also use a menu to apply this filter. Pull down the Effects menu and click Geometric Effects. In the submenu, click Cylinder - Horizontal or Cylinder - Vertical. Now complete the dialog in line with steps 1-2.

Re step 1 – the permitted range is 0-99.

Cylinder deformations in action:

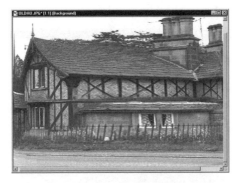

The Vertical Cylinder deformation

The Horizontal Cylinder deformation

Applying Cylinder deformations

Pull down the Effects menu and click Effect Browser. In the left column in the Browser, double-click Horizontal Cylinder or Vertical Cylinder. Do the following:

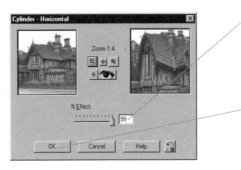

1 Specify a % effect

2 Click OK

The Pentagon deformation

The Rotating Mirror deformation reflects part of an image on itself

Follow step 1. In the Browser, double-click Rotating Mirror. Click OK. Complete the dialog then click OK.

The Pentagon deformation transforms an image into a five-sided figure.

After Pentagon has been applied

Rotating Mirror in action

Applying the Pentagon deformation

To apply this deformation via a menu route, ignore steps 2-4. Instead, pull down the Effects menu and select Geometric Effects, Pentagon.

1 Optional – to limit the deformation to part of the image, define the relevant selection area or mask

2 Pull down the Effects menu and select Effect Browser

3 Click Pentagon

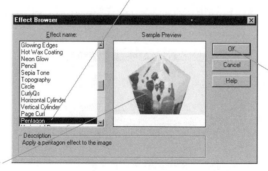

4 Click here

The result of applying the chosen deformation is previewed here:

The Perspective deformations

If you only want to apply the deformation to a part of the image, define a selection area first.

There are two perspective deformations. The Horizontal Perspective deformation slants an image horizontally, while the Vertical Perspective deformation slants it vertically.
The result incorporates a perspective effect.

Perspective deformations in action:

The Vertical Perspective deformation

The Horizontal Perspective deformation

You can also use a menu to apply this filter. Pull down the Effects menu and click Geometric Effects. In the submenu, click Perspective - Horizontal or Perspective - Vertical. Now complete the dialog in line with steps 1-2.

Applying Perspective deformations

Pull down the Effects menu and click Effect Browser. In the left column in the Browser, double-click Horizontal Perspective or Vertical Perspective. Do the following:

Re step 1 – the permitted range is -100 to +100.

1 Specify a % difference (between the shortened edge and the unaffected one)

2 Click OK

The Pinch deformation

Pinch compresses an image towards its centre.

You can apply the reverse of Pinch – Paint Shop Pro calls this Punch.

Follow steps 1-2. In step 3, double-click Punch. Complete the dialog in line with steps 4-5.

After Pinch has been applied

The same image, after Punch

Applying the Pinch deformation

1 Optional – to limit the deformation to part of the image, define the relevant selection area or mask

2 Pull down the Effects menu and select Effect Browser

To apply this deformation via a menu route, ignore steps 2-3. Instead, pull down the Effects menu and select Geometric Effects, Pinch. Now complete steps 4-5.

3 In the leftmost column in the Browser, double-click Pinch

4 Drag the slider to the required setting

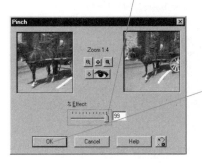

5 Click here

The Ripple deformation

Ripple defines concentric rings around (by default) an image's midpoint.

After Ripple has been applied

If you want to limit the deformation to a selection area or mask, define it before step 1.

To apply Twirl via a menu route, ignore steps 1-2. Instead, pull down the Effects menu and select Geometric Effects, Twirl. Complete steps 3-5.

Applying the Ripple deformation

1 Pull down the Effects menu and select Effect Browser

2 In the leftmost column in the Browser, double-click Ripple

Re step 3 – amplitude is the distance from the peak of each ripple to its base; wavelength is the distance between peaks.

3 Drag these sliders to specify the amplitude and wavelength

Re step 4 – these settings specify the ripple position relative to the image centre.

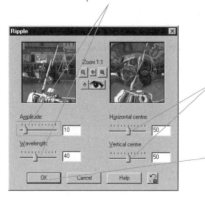

4 Drag these sliders to the required setting

5 Click here

The Skew deformation

The Skew deformation slants images.

Note that you can skew in two (mutually exclusive) directions:

• *vertically, or;*

• *horizontally*

Horizontal Skew in action

To apply this deformation via a menu route, ignore steps 2-3. Instead, pull down the Effects menu and select Geometric Effects, Skew. Now complete steps 4-5.

Applying the Skew deformation

1 Optional – to limit the deformation to part of the image, define the relevant selection area or mask

2 Pull down the Effects menu and select Effect Browser

3 In the leftmost column in the Browser, select Skew then click OK

You can also warp images by applying the Spiky Halo deformation (this applies a crown of waves arranged radially).
Follow steps 1-2. In step 3, double-click Spiky Halo. Complete the dialog then click OK.

4 Drag one of the sliders to the required setting

Spiky Halo in action

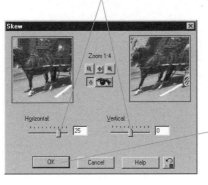

5 Click here

The Twirl deformation

The Twirl deformation rotates an image around its centre.

Twirl in action

If you want to limit the deformation to a selection area or mask, define it before step 1.

Applying the Twirl deformation

1 Pull down the Effects menu and select Effect Browser

2 In the leftmost column in the Browser, select Twirl then click OK

To apply this deformation via a menu route, ignore steps 1- 2. Instead, pull down the Effects menu and select Geometric Effects, Twirl. Now complete steps 3-4.

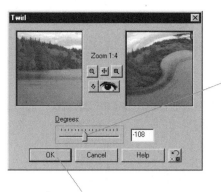

3 Drag the slider to specify the degree of Twirl

Re step 3 – minus settings produce an anti-clockwise rotation.

4 Click here

The Warp deformation

If you want to limit the deformation to a selection area or mask, define it before step 1.

To apply this deformation via a menu route, ignore steps 1-2. Instead, pull down the Effects menu and select Geometric Effects, Warp. Now complete steps 3-4.

The Warp deformation magnifies an image's centre in relation to the remainder.

Warp in action

Re step 3 – the strength is the degree of magnification; the size is self-explanatory.

Minus settings in the Strength field produce interesting results e.g.:

Applying the Warp deformation

1 Pull down the Effects menu and select Effect Browser

2 In the leftmost column in the Browser, select Warp then click OK

Also complete the fields in the Center Offset: section; these control the position of the deformation centre.

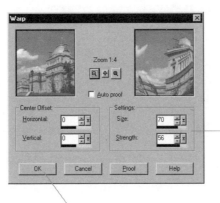

3 Specify the size and strength

4 Click here

The Wave deformation

If you want to limit the deformation to a selection area or mask, define it before step 1.

The Wave deformation imposes undulating vertical and horizontal lines.

The Wind deformation is another interesting effect you can apply.
Follow step 1. In step 2, double-click Wind. Complete the dialog then click OK.

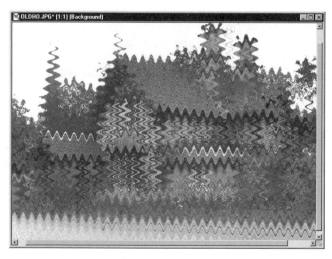

Wave in action

Applying the Wave deformation

1 Pull down the Effects menu and select Effect Browser

2 In the leftmost column in the Browser, select Wave then click OK

To apply Wave via a menu route, ignore steps 1-2. Instead, pull down the Effects menu and select Geometric Effects, Wave. Complete steps 3-4.

Re step 3 – the amplitude is the distance from the peak of each ripple to its base; the wavelength is the distance between each peak.

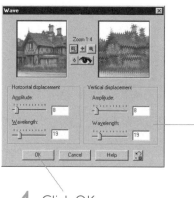

3 Specify the horizontal/ vertical amplitude and wavelength

4 Click OK

Using effects

In this chapter, you'll enhance images or image selections by applying any of Paint Shop Pro's numerous special effects. Some of these are especially useful for creating and designing Web sites (e.g. Buttonize and the ability to improve photographs) and they're flagged accordingly.

Covers

Chapter Six

The Black Pencil effect

Note that images must fall into the following categories:

- *coloured images with more than 256 colours, or;*
- *256-colour greyscales*

for effects to work on them. (If the image you want to apply an effect to doesn't meet these criteria, carry out the procedure in the HOT TIP on page 109.)

You can also activate this effect via the Effect Browser. Simply double-click its entry, then follow steps 3-4.

Experiment with applying more than one effect to images (or the same effect more than once) – the results can be dramatic.

Re step 3 – the Detail slider sets the number of strokes used; the Opacity slider determines the effect's intensity.

The Black Pencil effect mimics the result of drawing with a black pencil.

Black Pencil in action

Applying the Black Pencil effect

1 Optional – to restrict the effect, define a selection area

2 Pull down the Effect menu and select Artistic Effects, Black Pencil

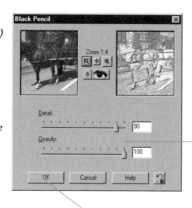

3 Drag the Detail & Opacity sliders to the required settings

4 Click here

The Blinds effect

The Blinds effect mimics the result of applying horizontal or vertical blinds.

 To specify a colour for the edges of the blinds, click the Colour: field. In the Colour dialog, select a new colour. Click OK.

 By default, blinds are lit from the bottom or right. To reverse this, select Light from left/top.

 You can also activate this effect via the Effect Browser. Simply double-click its entry, then follow steps 3-4.

 By default, blinds are horizontal. To make them vertical, deselect Horizontal.

 Re step 3 – the Width slider sets the blind width; the Opacity slider determines the effect's intensity.

Blinds in action

Applying the Blinds effect

1 Optional – to restrict the effect, define a selection area

2 Pull down the Effects menu and select Texture Effects, Blinds

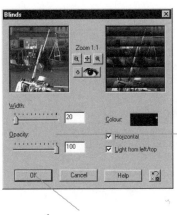

3 Drag the Width & Opacity sliders to the required settings

4 Click here

The Brush Strokes effect

Brush Strokes makes images resemble watercolours

The illustration below shows an image after Brush Strokes has been applied:

You can also activate this effect via the Effect Browser. Simply double-click its entry, then follow steps 3-4.

The 'Water colour' preset (intensified for effect)

Re step 3 – presets are ready-made formatting collections which give professional results. However, you can also omit step 3 and apply your own effect settings instead. For example:

- *to specify brush stroke length, complete the Strokes section of the dialog*
- *to specify the bristle number, complete the Brush section of the dialog*
- *to apply a coloured light, click in the Colour: box; in the list, select a colour and click OK*
- *to adjust the light origin, type in a new angle in the Angle: field*

Finally, when you've finished entering your own settings follow step 4.

Applying the Brush Strokes effect

1 Optional – to limit the effect to part of an image, define the relevant selection area

2 In the Effects menu, select Artistic Effects, Brush Strokes

3 Click here; in the list, select a preset

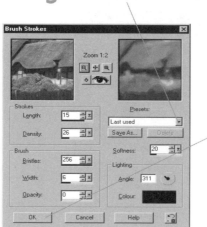

4 Click here

The Charcoal effect

The Charcoal effect resembles the Black Pencil effect; the difference is that it has more detail.

The Charcoal effect mimics the result of drawing with charcoal.

The illustration below shows an image after the Charcoal effect has been applied:

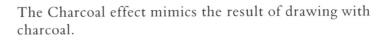

The Buttonize effect applies a raised 3-D border. Follow step 1. In step 2, select 3D Effects, Buttonize instead. Click OK. Complete the dialog then click OK.

Buttonize in action – use these on the Web

Applying the Charcoal effect

1 Optional – to restrict the effect, define a selection area

2 Pull down the Effects menu and select Artistic Effects, Charcoal

You can also activate this effect via the Effect Browser. Simply double-click its entry, then follow steps 3-4.

Re step 3 – the Detail slider sets the number of strokes used; the Opacity slider determines the effect's intensity.

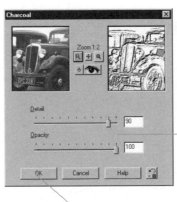

3 Drag the Detail & Opacity sliders to the required settings

4 Click here

The Chrome effect

The Chrome effect applies a metallic patina.

The illustration below shows an image after the Chrome effect has been applied:

You can make image selections appear to have been hewn out of stone:

First, define the relevant selection area. Pull down the Effects menu and click 3D Effects, Chisel. In the Chisel dialog, drag the Size slider to the required setting (to specify the extent of the chiselled area).
Finally, click OK.

Applying the Chrome effect

I   Optional – to restrict the effect, define a selection area

You can also activate the effects on this and the facing page via the Effect Browser. Simply double-click the relevant entry, then complete the dialog. Finally, click OK.

2   Pull down the Effects menu and select Artistic Effects, Chrome

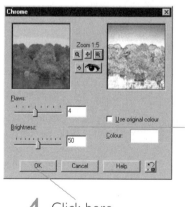

Re step 3 – the Flaws slider sets the number of creases (interactions between light and dark); the Brightness slider is self-explanatory.

3   Drag the Flaws & Brightness sliders to the required settings

4   Click here

The Coloured Chalk effect

You can combine a sculpted look with multiple colours:

Follow step 1. In step 2, click Artistic Effects, Coloured Foil in the Effects menu. In the dialog, select a preset. Carry out step 4.

The Coloured Chalk effect mimics the result of drawing with coloured chalk.

The illustration below shows an image after the Coloured Chalk effect has been applied:

You can also make an image look as if drawn with a coloured pencil:

Follow step 1, if applicable. In step 2, click Artistic Effects, Coloured Pencil in the Effects menu. Now carry out steps 3-4.

Applying the Coloured Chalk effect

1 Optional – to restrict the effect, define a selection area

2 In the Effects menu, select Artistic Effects, Coloured Chalk

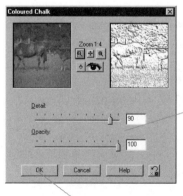

3 Drag the Detail & Opacity sliders to the required settings (the Detail slider sets the number of strokes used, the Opacity slider the effect's intensity)

4 Click here

The Contours effect

Contours changes images into topographical maps.

The illustration below shows an image after Contours has been applied:

The 'Ink Outline' preset

Applying the Contours effect

1 Optional – to limit the effect to part of an image, define the relevant selection area

2 In the Effects menu, select Artistic Effects, Contours

3 Click here; in the list, select a preset

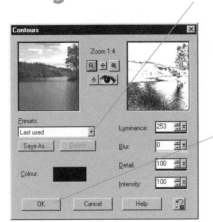

4 Click here

The Cutout effect

You can have Paint Shop Pro remove red-eye (the camera flash is reflected from the retina onto the film, making eyes look red) in photographs.

In the Effects menu, click Enhance Photo, Red-eye Removal. Complete the dialog (for instance, in the Method field, select a method e.g. Auto Human Eye) then click OK.

You can convert a selection area into a 'cutout'. You then have the impression of looking through the image to a recessed area.

The illustration below shows an image after the Cutout effect has been applied:

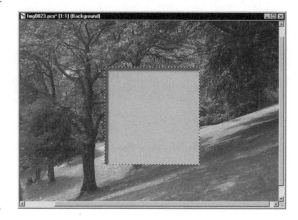

Re step 3 – if Fill interior with colour is selected, click in the Colour field to the right. In the Colour dialog, select a fill colour then click OK.

Applying the Cutout effect

1 Define the relevant selection area

2 Pull down the Effects menu and select 3D Effects, Cutout

Re step 4 – the Opacity slider determines the effect's intensity; the Blur slider widens and softens the cutout shadow.

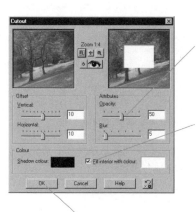

4 Drag the Opacity & Blur sliders to the required settings

3 Select Fill interior with colour if you don't want the cutout filled with the image

Also complete the fields in the Offset section; these control the position of the cutout's interior.

5 Click here

The Drop Shadow effect

The Drop Shadow effect only works with selection areas.

Drop Shadow imposes a shadow behind selection areas.

The illustration below shows an image after the Drop Shadow effect has been applied:

You can also activate this effect via the Effect Browser. Simply double-click its entry, then follow steps 3-4.

Applying the Drop Shadow effect

1 Define the relevant selection area

To apply a drop shadow to the whole of an image (as here), carry out the following extra procedures before step 1:

- *press Ctrl+A (to select the entire image), and;*

- *follow the procedures on page 17 to increase the image's canvas (so the shadow can display)*

2 Pull down the Effects menu and select 3D Effects, Drop Shadow

3 Drag the Vertical & Horizontal sliders to the required settings (to specify the shadow's position)

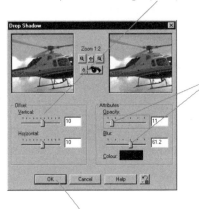

4 Drag the Opacity and Blur sliders to the required settings

Re step 4 – the Opacity slider sets the drop shadow density; the Blur slider determines its softness.

5 Click here

The Enamel effect

You can have Paint Shop Pro remove small scratches from photographs. Pull down the Effects menu and click Automatic Small Scratch Removal. In the dialog, select Remove dark scratches or Remove light scratches, as appropriate. Select a strength (Mild, Normal or Aggressive) then a contrast limit. Finally, click OK.

Enamel applies a shiny coating to images.

The illustration below shows an image after Enamel has been applied:

You can also activate this effect via the Effect Browser. Simply double-click its entry, then follow steps 3-4.

Re step 3 – consider amending the dialog in line with these guidelines:

- *to specify image sharpness and relief scale, complete the fields in the Relief section*

- *to apply a coloured light, click in the Colour: box; in the list, select a colour and click OK*

- *to adjust the light origin, type in a new angle in the Angle: field*

Finally, when you've finished entering your own settings follow step 4.

Applying the Enamel effect

1 Optional – to restrict the effect, define a selection area

2 Pull down the Effects menu and select Artistic Effects, Enamel

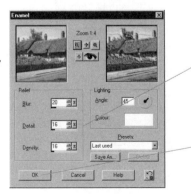

3 Complete the fields in the Relief section

4 Click OK

The Feedback effect

The Feedback effect makes an image appear to be reflected inwards in a series of concentric mirrors.

The illustration below shows an image after the Feedback effect has been applied:

Applying the Feedback effect

1 Optional – to restrict the effect, define a selection area

2 Pull down the Effects menu and select Reflection Effects, Feedback

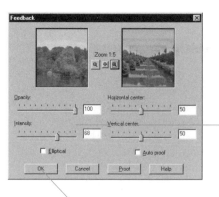

3 Drag the Opacity & Intensity sliders to the required settings

4 Click here

The Fur effect

Fur makes images appear bristly.

The illustration below shows an image after Fur has been applied:

You can also activate this effect via the Effect Browser. Simply double-click its entry, then follow steps 3-4.

Applying the Fur effect

Re step 3 – consider amending the dialog in line with these guidelines:

- the Blur field specifies image sharpness
- the Density field specifies effect intensity
- the Length field specifies bristle length
- the Transparency field specifies image visibility

Finally, when you've finished entering your own settings follow step 4.

1   Optional – to restrict the effect, define a selection area

2   Pull down the Effects menu and select Texture Effects, Fur

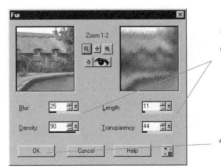

3   Complete the relevant fields in line with the HOT TIP

4   Click OK

The Glowing Edges effect

The Glowing Edges effect colours image edges in neon (other image parts are blackened).

The illustration below shows an image after the Glowing Edges effect has been applied:

You can also activate this effect via the Effect Browser. Simply double-click its entry, then follow steps 3-4.

To apply a 3-D effect to the interior of a selection area, first define the area. Pull down the Effects menu and choose 3D Effects, Inner Bevel. Click in the Presets: field in the Inner Bevel dialog; in the list, select a preset bevel effect.
Finally, click OK.

Applying the Glowing Edges effect

1 Optional – to restrict the effect, define a selection area

2 Pull down the Effects menu and select Artistic Effects, Glowing Edges

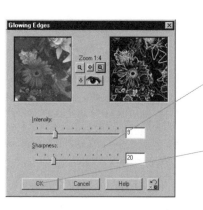

Re step 3 – the Intensity slider controls edge brightness; the Sharpness slider is self-explanatory.

3 Drag the Intensity & Sharpness sliders to the required settings

4 Click OK

The Kaleidoscope effect

When you apply the Kaleidoscope effect, Paint Shop Pro defines a (loosely) pie-shaped area at the centre of the image; this is surrounded by a circular pattern.

(The setting specified by step 3 controls the width of the outer edge.)

The Kaleidoscope effect mimics looking at an image through a kaleidoscope.

The illustration below shows an image after the Kaleidoscope effect has been applied:

You can also activate this effect via the Effect Browser. Simply double-click its entry, then follow steps 3-4.

Applying the Kaleidoscope effect

I Optional – to restrict the effect, define a selection area

2 Pull down the Effects menu and select Reflection Effects, Kaleidoscope

Also complete the fields in the Image Sector section; these control which portion of the image is used to create the outer circle.

Entering a value in the Radial Suction: field specifies the place in the inner pie from which Paint Shop Pro derives its pattern data.

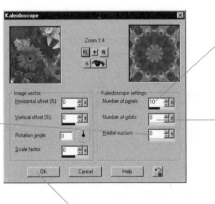

3 Specify the number of petals

4 Optional – specify the number of pattern repeats

5 Click here

The Lights effect

You can also activate this effect via the Effect Browser. Simply double-click its entry, then follow steps 3-4.

You can have Paint Shop Pro appear to view images via a camera lens.

Follow step 1. In step 2, click Illumination Effects, Sunburst in the Effects menu. In the dialog, select a preset. Carry out step 4.

Lights spotlights images (with up to five spotlights).

The illustration below shows an image after Lights has been applied:

The 'Flood' preset

Applying the Lights effect

1 Optional – to limit the effect to part of an image, define the relevant selection area

2 In the Effects menu, select Illumination Effects, Lights

3 Click here; in the list, select a preset

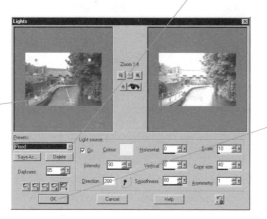

Re step 3 – you can omit this step and apply your own settings instead. For example, to fine-tune the effect, drag any screen element here to a new location:

Finally, when you've finished entering your own settings follow step 4.

4 Click here

The Mosaic - Antique effect

You can also tile images with glass:

Follow step 1, as applicable. In step 2, select Texture Effects, Mosaic - Glass. Now carry out steps 3-4.

You can also activate this effect via the Effect Browser. Simply double-click its entry, then follow steps 3-4.

Optionally, also complete the fields in the Grid Settings section:

- *Tile Opacity – specifies how much of the underlying image shows through*
- *Grout Width – specifies the gap between tiles, and;*
- *Grout Opacity – specifies the opacity of the gap between tiles*

The Mosaic - Antique effect mimics applying antique tiles to an image.

The illustration below shows an image after the Mosaic - Antique effect has been applied:

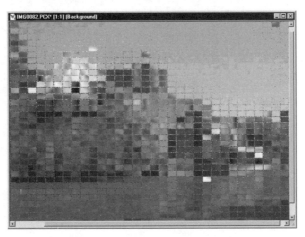

Applying the Mosaic - Antique effect

1 Optional – to restrict the effect, define a selection area

2 Pull down the Effects menu and select Geometric Effects, Mosaic - Antique

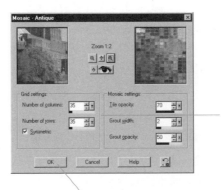

3 Specify the number of columns and rows

4 Click here

The Neon Glow effect

Neon Glow mimics applying neon colours to an image.

The illustration below shows an image after the Neon Glow effect has been applied:

To apply a 3-D effect to part of an image, define the relevant selection area. Pull down the Effects menu and choose 3D Effects, Outer Bevel. Click in the Presets: field in the Outer Bevel dialog; in the list, select a preset bevel effect.

Finally, click OK.

Applying the Neon Glow effect

1 Optional – to restrict the effect, define a selection area

You can also activate this effect via the Effect Browser. Simply double-click its entry, then follow steps 3-4.

2 Pull down the Effects menu and select Artistic Effects, Neon Glow

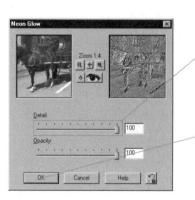

Re step 3 – the Detail slider sets the number (and brightness) of colours used; the Opacity slider determines the effect's intensity.

3 Drag the Detail & Opacity sliders to the required settings

4 Click OK

The Page Curl effect

Page Curl rolls up one image corner.

The illustration below shows an image after Page Curl has been applied:

You can also activate this effect via the Effect Browser. Simply double-click its entry, then follow steps 3-4.

Re step 3 – consider amending the dialog in line with these guidelines:

- the Back colour: field specifies the colour for the area underneath the curl – left-click it and select the colour you want

- the Colour field: specifies the colour of the curl back – left-click it and select the colour you want

- the icons in the Corner field select which corner is curled

- drag the bar here: to amend the curl start and/or end points

Finally, when you've finished entering your own settings follow step 4.

Applying the Page Curl effect

1 Optional – to restrict the effect, define a selection area

2 In the Effects menu, select Geometric Effects, Page Curl

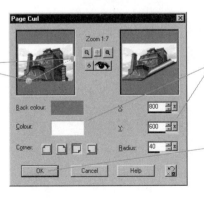

3 Amend the dialog in line with the HOT TIP

4 Click OK

The Pattern effect

The Pattern effect creates patterns from any image.

The illustration below shows an image after the Pattern effect has been applied:

You can also activate the effects on this and the facing page via the Effect Browser. Simply double-click the relevant entry, then complete the dialog. Finally, click OK.

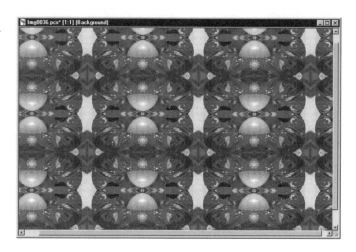

Applying the Pattern effect

I   Optional – to restrict the effect, define a selection area

2   In the Effects menu, select Reflection Effects, Pattern

Optionally, also complete the fields in the Image Area: section:

- *The Offset fields – specify where the pattern begins (the default is the image centre)*
- *Rotation Angle – to rotate the effect, enter the relevant angle, and;*
- *Scale Factor – specifies pattern size (the smaller the pattern, the more it repeats)*

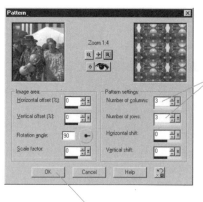

3   Specify the number of rows/columns

4   Click here

The Pencil effect

You can have Paint Shop Pro impose a terrace-like effect on images.

The Pencil effect turns images into pencil drawings.

The illustration below shows an image after the Pencil effect has been applied:

Follow step 1. In step 2, click Artistic Effects, Topography in the Effects menu. Complete the dialog then carry out step 4.

Applying the Pencil effect

1 Optional – to restrict the effect, define a selection area

Optionally, also complete the fields in the Image Area: section:

2 In the Effects menu, select Artistic Effects, Pencil

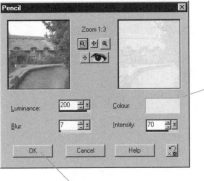

- to vary the light applied, click in the Colour: box; in the list, select a colour and click OK

- to brighten or darken the image, amend the Luminance field

- to amend image sharpness, amend the Blur field (higher values produce less sharpness)

- to view more detail, increase the value in the Intensity field

3 Complete the relevant fields – see the DON'T FORGET tip

4 Click here

The Polished Stone effect

Polished Stone makes images appear to have been carved out of a shiny stone.

The illustration below shows an image after the Polished Stone effect has been applied:

The 'Custom' preset

Applying the Polished Stone effect

*Re step 3 –
You can omit
step 3 and
apply your own
effect settings
instead. For example:*

- *enter a new value in the Blur: field to specify image sharpness*
- *enter a new value in the Detail: field to specify relief scale*
- *enter a new value in the Polishing: field to specify the size of the polished section*
- *to adjust the light origin, type in a new angle in the Angle: field*
- *to apply a coloured light, click in the Colour: box – in the list, select a colour and click OK*

Finally, when you've finished entering your own settings follow step 4.

1 Optional – to limit the effect to part of an image, define the relevant selection area

2 In the Effects menu, select Texture Effects, Polished Stone

3 Click here; in the list, select a preset

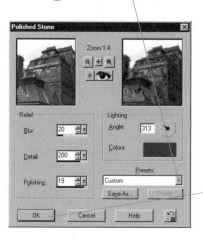

4 Click here

The Sculpture effect

The Sculpture effect combines embossing with the application of a coloured pattern.

The illustration below shows an image after the Sculpture effect has been applied:

You can also activate the effects on this and the facing page via the Effect Browser. Simply double-click the relevant entry, then complete the dialog. Finally, click OK.

Re step 3 – you can omit step 3 and apply your own effect settings instead. For example:

- *to apply a new background pattern, click in the Pattern: box; in the list, select a new one*
- *to apply a coloured light, click in the Colour: box; in the list, select a colour and click OK*
- *to customise the sculpture itself, amend the fields in the Image section*
- *to adjust the light origin, type in a new angle in the Angle: field*

Finally, when you've finished entering your own settings follow step 4.

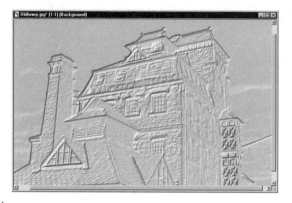

The 'Gold' preset

Applying the Sculpture effect

1 Optional – to limit the effect to part of an image, define the relevant selection area

2 In the Effects menu, select Texture Effects, Sculpture

3 Click here; in the list, select a preset

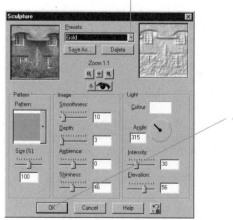

4 Click here

The Texture effect

You can make greyscale or 16 million colour images appear to have been embossed on leather.

Texture mimics painting an image onto a textured medium.

The illustration below shows an image after Texture has been applied:

The 'Wrinkled' preset

Pull down the Effects menu and click Texture Effects, Rough Leather. Select a preset and/or complete the other dialog fields. Click OK.

Applying the Texture effect

Re step 3 – You can omit step 3 and apply your own effect settings instead. For example:

- *to apply a new texture, click in the Texture: box; in the list, select a new one (then, optionally, resize it)*

- *to apply a coloured light, click in the Colour: box; in the list, select a colour and click OK*

- *to customise the sculpture itself, amend the fields in the Image section*

- *to adjust the light origin, type in a new angle in the Angle: field*

Finally, when you've finished entering your own settings follow step 4.

1 Optional – to limit the effect to part of an image, define the relevant selection area

2 In the Effects menu, select Texture Effects, Texture

3 Click here; in the list, select a preset

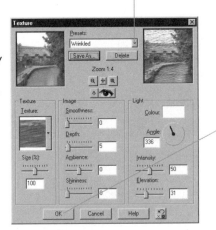

4 Click here

The Tiles effect

Tiles makes an image look as if it was created from tiles.

The illustration below shows a bitmap rectangle after the Tiles effect has been applied:

You can also activate the effects on this and the facing page via the *Effect Browser*. Simply double-click the relevant entry, then complete the dialog. Finally, click OK.

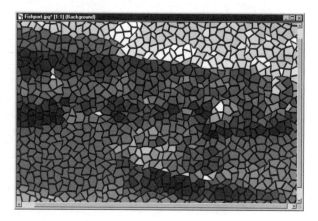

The 'Stained Glass' preset

Re step 3 – you can omit step 3 and apply your own effect settings instead. For example:

- to apply a new tile, click in the Tile shape: box; in the list, select a new one (then, optionally, customise the angularity/ size)
- to apply a coloured light, click in the Colour: box; in the list, select a colour and click OK
- to customise the tiling itself, amend the fields in the Image section
- to adjust the light origin, type in a new angle in the Angle: field

Finally, when you've finished entering your own settings follow step 4.

Applying the Tiles effect

1 Optional – to limit the effect to part of an image, define the relevant selection area

2 In the Effects menu, select Texture Effects, Tiles

3 Click here; in the list, select a preset

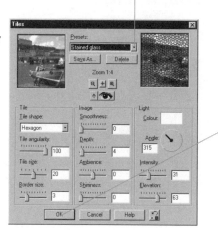

4 Click here

The Weave effect

You can also activate this effect via the Effect Browser. Simply double-click its entry, then follow steps 3-4.

Weave applies a basketwork effect to images.

The illustration below shows an image after applying Weave:

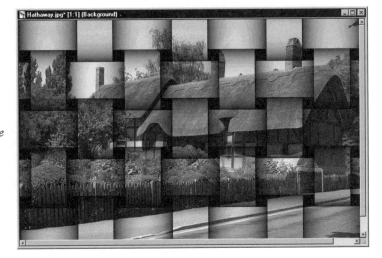

If you want the gap between strands to be filled with the image (rather than a colour), deselect Fill gaps.

By default, the weave colour is black. To apply a new one, click the Weave colour: field. In the Colour dialog, select it, then click OK.

Applying the Weave effect

1 Optional – to restrict the effect, define a selection area

2 In the Effects menu, select Texture Effects, Weave

To specify the gap between strands, drag the Gap size: slider to the correct setting.

Re step 3 – the Width slider sets the thickness of each individual strand; the Opacity slider determines the effect's intensity.

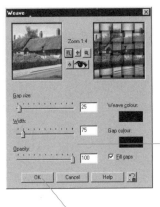

3 Drag the Width & Opacity sliders to the required settings

4 Click here

Advanced techniques

In this chapter, you'll learn how to apply borders/frames to images; carry out screen captures; work with layers; and apply/edit masks. You'll also create workspaces (so you can return more quickly to ongoing work) and use Autosave (to guard against system crashes). Then you'll crop images; work with histograms to readjust colour values; and carry out other colour corrections (including Posterize/Solarize). Finally, you'll convert images in batches, then preview – and print – your work (including multiple image printing).

Covers

Chapter Seven

Layers – an overview

You can paint (or apply effects to) specific layers. When you do this, unaffected areas in underlying layers remain visible until such time as you merge the layers.

Paint Shop Pro images are divided into 'layers'. Layers are separate, transparent levels which add a new dimension to image editing. Memory permitting, you can have as many as 100 layers.

There are three kinds of layer:

- Raster (hosts pixel-related data)

- Vector (holds vector objects e.g. shapes and text)

- Adjustment (contains colour correction data)

Much of the usefulness of layers comes from the following:

- making one or more layers temporarily invisible

- applying masks to layers (see later)

Vector layers can be added to any image, but Raster and Adjustment layers can only be created in:

- greyscale images

- images with at least 16 million colours

Layer editing and manipulation are largely undertaken via the Layer palette. The Layer palette shows each layer and its sequence in the overall stack of layers. It also, in the case of a vector layer, displays icons representing each vector object:

To the left of the button which displays the layer name, Paint Shop Pro displays an icon showing what type of layer it is e.g.:

Bitmap

Vector

Background

The icon for Adjustment layers varies with the sub-type.

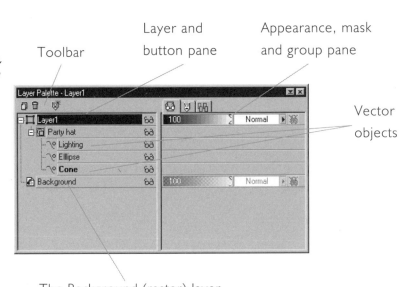

Toolbar

Layer and button pane

Appearance, mask and group pane

Vector objects

The Background (raster) layer – each new image has one

Adding new layers

1 In the Layer palette toolbar (see the facing page), right-click this button:

You can use a shortcut to create a new raster layer (with default properties): hold down Shift as you click this button in the Layer palette toolbar:

2 Click a layer type

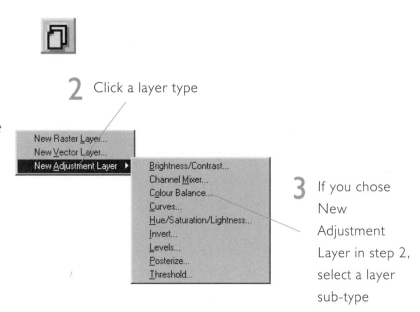

3 If you chose New Adjustment Layer in step 2, select a layer sub-type

To launch the Layer palette, right-click any toolbar. In the menu, select *Layer Palette*.
(Or, as a shortcut, simply press L.)

4 Name the layer

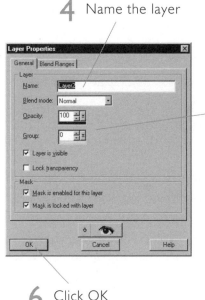

5 Complete the remaining fields (they vary according to the layer type) or accept the defaults

6 Click OK

Using layers

Rearranging layers

I If the Layer palette isn't on-screen, press L

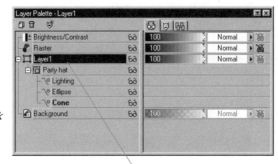

To delete a layer, right-click it in the Layer palette. In the menu which launches, click Delete.

2 Click a layer, then drag it up or down to a new location in the palette

3 Release the mouse button

Merging layers

When you merge layers, you join all the component layers (or simply all visible layers) into one. As a result:

By default, each image has a Background layer. To promote this into a normal one, right-click it in the palette. In the menu, select Promote To Layer.

• they can no longer be edited independently

• all vector objects are rasterised

• all transparent areas are whitened

Carry out ONE of the following, as appropriate:

To retain all layer information, follow the procedures in the HOT TIP on page 18 when saving your layered images.

However, note that you can also select 'Photoshop (*.psd)' in step 1 on page 18 since the Adobe Photoshop format also retains full layer details.

I To merge all the layers within an image, pull down the Layers menu and select Merge All (Flatten)

2 To merge only those layers currently visible within an image, pull down the Layers menu and select Merge Visible

...cont'd

You can border images with the Background colour. You can border all four sides, or permutations.

Open the relevant image. Pull down the Image menu and select Add Borders. Now do one of the following:

* *in the dialog, leave Symmetric selected to border all sides, then enter a border thickness in one of the entry fields.*

* *alternatively, to only border specific sides, deselect Symmetric and enter a thickness in one or more fields.*

Finally, click OK.

A framed picture

To frame an image, pull down the Image menu and click Picture Frame. Complete the Picture Frame Wizard dialogs.

Duplicating layers

| If the Layer palette isn't on-screen, press L

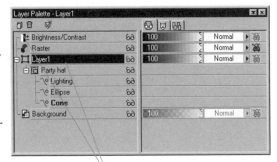

2 Click a layer, then drag it over the button

3 Release the mouse button

The result:

The Background layer has been copied (the new layer is named 'Copy of ...')

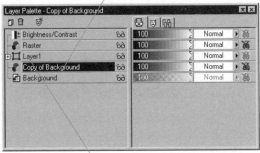

For illustration purposes, the components of the vector layer (Layer I) have been hidden by clicking here: The minus box becomes: **+**

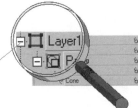

Viewing layers

To re-display a layer, repeat step 2 but click this icon instead:

Hiding/showing layers

1 If the Layer palette isn't on-screen, press L

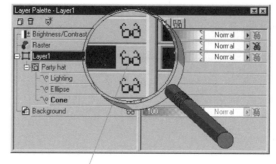

To view or hide all layers, pull down the Layers menu and click View, All or View, None respectively.

2 Click a layer's Visibility button to hide it – the button changes to:

To make all invisible layers visible (or vice versa), pull down the Layers menu and click View, Invert.

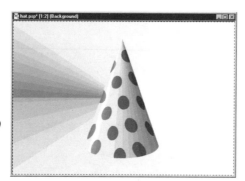

Here, 2 layers are shown: 1 gradient background (raster) and 1 vector (the hat)

Current (visible) layers which hold no data are transparent.

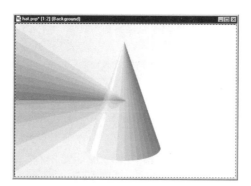

Now, 2 vector objects (Ellipse and Cone) have been hidden

Masks – an overview

The fact that masks are bitmaps means that all bitmap tools work with them.

Another corollary is that in those tools which have bitmap and vector modes (e.g. the Preset Shapes tool), only the bitmap component is operative on masks.

Masks are 256-colour greyscale bitmaps which are overlaid over image layers. They contain 'holes'; you perform editing operations on the areas displayed through the gaps. The holes can be created via:

• selection areas

• other images

Alternatively, the mask can be as large as the underlying layer.

To an extent, as we've seen, masks can be regarded as stencils. However, also implicit in the above description is the fact that they act as advanced selection areas. For example, you can control the extent to which a mask operates by defining the greyscale content:

You can apply any filter, deformation or effect which can be used with greyscale images.

— painting with black augments masking

— painting with white effaces masking

— any intervening shade of grey allows a portion of the effect you generate to take effect

In the illustration on the right, a separate image has been applied as a mask, and a fill applied

Layer masks

You shouldn't apply masks to a Background layer – instead, promote the layer first. (See the HOT TIP on page 168.)

You can create three principal types of mask:

- masks which apply to one specific layer

- selection masks (formed from, and based on, a pre-defined selection)

- image masks (based on a second image)

Masking an entire layer

| If the Layer palette isn't on-screen, press L

If the Layer palette isn't on-screen, right-click the Toolbar and select Layer Palette.

Toolbar

Layer Palette Copy of Background			
Brightness/Contrast	⑥⑥	100	Normal ▶ ✕
Raster	⑥⑥	100	Normal ▶ ✕
Layer1	⑥⑥	100	Normal ▶ ✕
Copy of Background	⑥⑥	100	Normal ▶ ✕
Background	⑥⑥	100	Normal ▶ ✕

2 Select a layer

Re steps 3 and 4 – you can edit the mask later to mask selective areas.

3 Left-click this button: 👹 in the Layer palette's toolbar – the entire layer is now masked

4 To unmask the layer, select it in the Layer palette. Pull down the Masks menu and click Delete. In the message which appears, click No to remove the mask entirely or Yes to incorporate it into the layer

Selection masks

When you create a mask, it's invisible. To view it, press Ctrl+Alt+V. (To hide it again, repeat this.) Viewed masks are coloured red:

Selection masks are masks which contain a hole (the hole being supplied by the selection area). By default, any changes you make apply to the hole, not the surrounding area.

Creating a selection mask

Define the appropriate selection area (see chapter 2 for how to do this). Now do the following:

1 If the Layer palette isn't on-screen, press L

A rectangular selection mask made visible

Toolbar

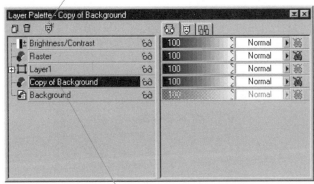

2 Select the relevant layer

3 Right-click this button: in the Layer palette's toolbar, then do ONE of the following:

After step 5, press Ctrl+D to remove the original selection area.

4 In the menu, click Hide Selection (to mask the selection)

5 In the menu, click Show Selection (to mask everything apart from the selection)

Image masks

Creating masks from other images is a very useful technique. It can produce quite remarkable effects.

Creating masks from images

1 Open the image you want to use as a mask

2 Open the image into which you want to insert the mask

3 In the destination image, follow steps 1-2 on page 173

4 Pull down the Masks menu and click New, From Image

5 Click here; in the list, select the mask image

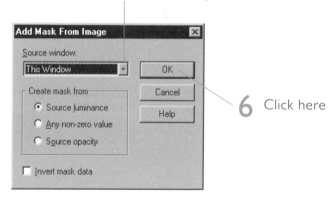

6 Click here

The result:

One image (the helicopter) has been inserted over another as a mask

Editing masks

In particular, you can use the Fill tool to apply a new fill. (See page 171 for a description of how colours influence the efficiency of masks.)

Paint Shop Pro has a special mode in which you can edit masks. This can involve:

- varying the extent of the mask (i.e. by painting over the object)

- painting the mask to control the degree (if any) of masking

Amending a mask

1 To view the mask, pull down the Masks menu and select View Mask

2 To enter Edit mode, press Ctrl+K

Re step 3 — you should make use of the following as guidelines:

- *paint with black to add masking*
- *paint with white to remove the mask, or;*
- *paint with grey shades to apply differing mask levels*

3 Alter the mask with any of the painting tools

4 To leave Edit mode, press Ctrl+K again

Reusing masks

Paint Shop Pro lets you save a mask to disk, as a special file (with the suffix .MSK). You can then load it into a new image. This is a convenient way to reuse masks.

Saving a mask

Define a mask. Pull down the Masks menu and click Save To Disk. Now do the following:

Re step 2 – you may have to activate one or more folders first, to locate the folder you want to save the mask to.

It's probably best to use 'Masks':

Click here. In the drop-down list, click a drive

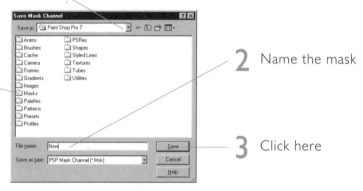

2 Name the mask

3 Click here

Loading a mask

Pull down the Masks menu and click Load From Disk. Now do the following:

Click here. In the drop-down list, click a drive

Re step 2 – you may have to activate one or more folders first, to locate the folder which hosts the mask you want to open.

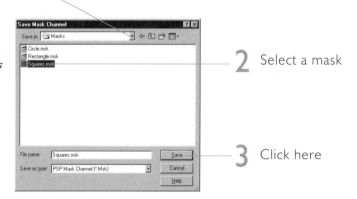

2 Select a mask

3 Click here

Screen captures

In programs (like Word 2000) which support OLE (Object Linking and Embedding), you can capture screens without having already started Paint Shop Pro.

In the OLE-compliant program, activate the 'Insert Object' command (usually Insert Object in the Insert menu). In the dialog, activate the Create New tab/ feature and double-click Paint Shop Pro 7 Screen Capture. Follow steps 1-3 on page 178, then click OK. Go to the screen you want to capture and follow step D. on the right.

The captured screen is inserted into the OLE-compliant program.

You can correct fade (the process by which light distorts the colours) in photographs.
Pull down the Effects menu and click Enhance Photo, Fade Correction.

Type in a correction amount (in the range 1-100) then click OK

You can have Paint Shop Pro create a snapshot of all or part of any Windows screen.

You can:

• specify which part of the screen is captured

• specify the signal which initiates the capture. You can use:

— a keystroke combination (known as a 'hotkey') – e.g. F11 or Alt+F1

— the right mouse button

— a specific interval (in seconds) instead of a trigger

• include the cursor in the capture

Having Paint Shop Pro perform a screen capture consists of the following sequential stages:

A. arranging the screen appropriately (this includes making the program whose screen you want to capture active)

B. switching to Paint Shop Pro

C. telling Paint Shop Pro to initiate a capture (at which point it minimises)

D. issue the capture signal

E. returning to Paint Shop Pro (the captured screen automatically occupies its own window) and performing any necessary editing actions (e.g. cropping or converting to greyscale)

F. using standard procedures to save the screen capture as a graphics file for later use

Re step 2 – you can dispense with allocating a trigger and, instead, tell Paint Shop Pro to begin the capture process so many seconds after you carry out step 4.

Simply omit step 2 and select Delay timer. Now insert the relevant interval into the box below Delay timer.

Performing a screen capture

Perform steps A-B on page 177. Pull down the File menu and click Import, Screen Capture, Setup. Do the following:

1 Select a region   2 Optional – select a trigger

3 Optional – ensure this is selected (see the tip)

4 Click here

Re step 3 – carry out this step if you want to capture the cursor e.g.:

Paint Shop Pro's Zoom cursor

(You can't capture the cursor if you selected Area in step 1.)

Paint Shop Pro minimises, and you're returned to the application whose screen you want to capture. Now perform ONE of the following:

5 If you selected Area, Object, Window or Client area in step 1, place the cursor over the screen component you want to capture

6 If you selected Full Screen in step 1, place the cursor anywhere on the screen

Follow step D on page 177. Additionally, if you selected Area in step 1 above:

7 Position the cursor at one corner of the area you want to capture. Left-click once, then place the cursor at the opposing corner and left-click again

Back in Paint Shop Pro, perform steps E and F on page 177, as appropriate.

Colour corrections – an overview

You can 'crop' images. This means defining an area you want to keep and discarding the rest.

Define the relevant selection area, then press Shift+R.

Alternatively, activate the Crop tool:

Define the relevant selection area, then double-click inside it.

You can use the Crop tool (see the above tip) to adjust the crop area you've just defined.

- *to move (but not resize) the crop rectangle, click inside it and drag to a new location, or;*
- *to resize the rectangle, move the cursor over one of the sides or corners, then drag in or out*

To convert a colour image to greyscale, pull down the Colours menu and click Grey Scale.

Paint Shop Pro lets you make various adjustments to image colour distribution. To help you decide which amendments are necessary, you can call up a special window: the Histogram viewer. Look at the illustrations below:

The original image

Spike

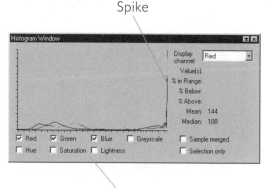

And its histogram (to launch the Histogram window, press H)

Here, the RGB (Red/Green/Blue) components have been selected

The Histogram window displays, along the horizontal axis, the three RGB components (Red, Green and Blue). The vertical axis against which these are plotted represents each component's share of colours.

The far left of the horizontal axis represents black, the far right white. The 'spike' at the right of the histogram occurs because of the predominance of the sky in the illustration.

Histogram functions

To invert an image (convert its colours to their opposites), pull down the Colours menu and click Negative Image.

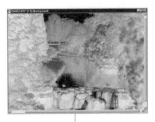

The higher image on the right, inverted

You can carry out two histogram-based operations on images: Equalize and Stretch.

Equalize rearranges image pixels so that those around the midpoint of the relevant histogram are pushed nearer the high and low brightness levels (see page 179 for more information). The result is normally an averaging of image brightness.

Stretch has somewhat the opposite effect. In images where black and white are not included in the histogram, it ensures the colours do span the full spectrum.

Applying Equalize or Stretch

If appropriate, define a selection area. Pull down the Colours menu and click Histogram Functions, Equalize OR Histogram Functions, Stretch.

To carry out a variety of further colour adjustments (e.g. amend brightness/contrast), pull down the Colours menu and click Adjust, followed by the relevant sub-option. Complete the dialog which launches, and click OK.

You can also automate the process to some extent. Choose Enhance Photo in the Effects menu, then click Automatic Colour Balance, Automatic Contrast Enhancement or Automatic Saturation Enhancement. Complete the dialog and click OK.

An unchanged image

And after applying Equalize

Solarize

Solarize inverts (reverses) colours which are over a user-set luminance threshold.

Paint Shop Pro has two further functions which manipulate image colours: Solarize and Posterize.

The illustration below shows the effect of applying the Solarize effect to the image on the facing page:

To Posterize an image (where you specify an image's brightness value so that the result amounts to a special effect), pull down the Colours menu and select Posterize. In the dialog, amend the Levels field (in the range 2-255, where 2 produces the maximum effect). Click OK.

Posterize in action (maximum effect)

Solarizing an image

1 Optional – to restrict the effect, define a selection area

2 Pull down the Colours menu and select Solarize

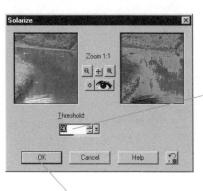

Setting the threshold at 1 is the same as inversion (see the HOT TIP on the facing page).

3 Drag the Threshold slider to the required setting – the permitted range is 1 (maximal effect) to 254 (minimal effect)

4 Click here

Using workspaces

You can save details of:

- toolbar and palette placement (i.e. whether they're docked or floating and – if floating – where they are on screen)

- grid and ruler settings

- which images are active and where their files are stored

- current zoom settings

as a 'workspace' file to disk. Paint Shop Pro gives the files a .WSP extension.

The advantage of this procedure is that you can quickly and easily return to a previous configuration of Paint Shop Pro, simply by loading the appropriate workspace file.

You should note the following when you create a workspace:

- *Paint Shop Pro prompts you to save any previously unsaved (and therefore unnamed) images*

- *Paint Shop Pro automatically saves any previously saved images which have since been amended*

- *the workspace save only stores details of where the relevant files are located, not the files themselves (this means that if you move or delete any of the files, they will not be present when you reload the workspace)*

Saving workspaces

1 Pull down the File menu and click Workspace, Save

2 Select a drive/folder

3 Name the workspace

4 Click Save

In chapter 1, we looked at saving images to alternative formats. This is a way of converting images, but one at a time. However, Paint Shop Pro lets you convert multiple images in one operation, a great saving in time and effort.

Pull down the File menu and click Batch Conversion. Use the Batch Conversion dialog to:

- *locate the files you want to convert*

- *select them (hold down Shift and click to select ranges)*

- *select an output format*

- *(optionally) customise the output format (by clicking the Options button and completing the resultant format-variable dialog)*

- *select an output folder*

Click Start to perform the conversion. When Paint Shop Pro tells you conversion is complete, click OK.

Recently saved workspaces can also be loaded via a menu. Pull down the File menu and click Workspace. In the sub-menu, click the workspace entry.

Loading workspaces

| Pull down the File menu and click Workspace, Save

2 Select a drive/folder

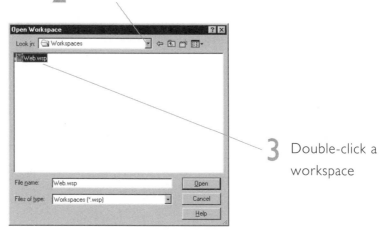

3 Double-click a workspace

Deleting workspaces

| Pull down the File menu and click Workspace, Delete

2 Select a drive/folder

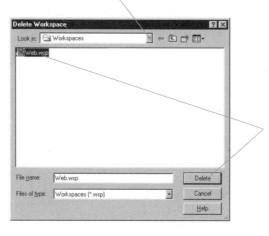

3 Click a workspace then click Delete

Using Autosave

If Windows or Paint Shop Pro crash suddenly, you run the risk of losing much or all of your work. However, you can prevent this by activating Paint Shop Pro's Autosave feature. When active, Autosave stores temporary details of active images. After any crash, Paint Shop Pro searches for these when you restart it. If it finds them, it reloads the temporary images.

Activating Autosave

Pull down the File menu and click Preferences, Autosave Settings.

To deactivate Autosave, deselect Enable autosave.

Select Enable autosave

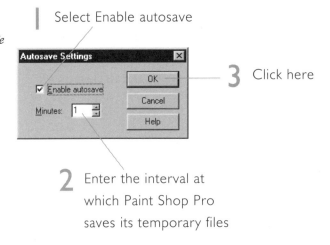

3 Click here

2 Enter the interval at which Paint Shop Pro saves its temporary files

By default, Paint Shop Pro saves its temporary files in your \WINDOWS\TEMP folder. However, you can change this if you want.

Specifying a new temporary file location

You'll have to restart Windows before this change takes effect.

1 Pull down the File menu and click Preferences, File Locations

2 In the File Locations dialog, activate the Undo/Temporary Files tab

3 In the Location of undo/temporary files box, type in the new folder address then click OK

Using Print Preview

To specify page setup settings, click this button in the toolbar:

Setup...

Make the relevant amendments in the Page Setup dialog. For example:

- *to print in greyscale (not colour), select Greyscale*
- *to centre the image on the page, select Center on page*
- *to print lengthways (not vertically), select Landscape*
- *to select a page size, click in the Size field; in the list, select a size, and/or;*
- *to use another printer, click the Printer button, select it in the new dialog then click OK*

Finally, click OK.

Paint Shop Pro provides a special view mode called Print Preview. This displays the active image exactly as it will look when printed. Use Print Preview as a final check just before you print your image.

You can customise the way Print Preview displays your image by zooming in or out on the active page. You can also specify page setup settings.

Launching Print Preview
Pull down the File menu and click Print Preview. This is the result:

Print Preview toolbar

Zooming in and out in Print Preview
To zoom in (increase magnification), click this button:

Zoom In   Repeat if necessary

To zoom out, click this button:

Zoom Out   Repeat if necessary

Printing

When you've previewed your image and it's ready to print, do the following:

Printing your work

Pull down the File menu and carry out the following steps:

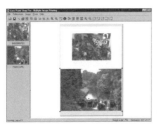

do the following:

- *drag images from the bar on the left onto the correct page location (as here)*
- *(optionally) click an image and apply any relevant menu commands (e.g. to view information about the image, select Image Information in the Image menu...)*
- *finally, to print the images pull down the File menu and click Print*

Click Print

2 Click here; select a printer

3 Optional – click here to adjust your printer's settings

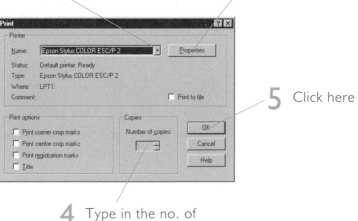

5 Click here

4 Type in the no. of copies you require

Paint Shop Pro starts printing the active image.

Index